Tasty
Low-fat
RECIPES

The Confident Cooking Promise of Success

Welcome to the world of Confident Cooking,
where recipes are double-tested by our team
of home economists to achieve a high standard
of success—and delicious results every time.

D1517476

bay books

C O N T E

Mediterranean fish soup, page 14

Moussaka, page 20

Chicken pies, page 46

Lamb cutlets with cannellini purée, page 37

Seafood and herb risotto, page 60

The Publisher thanks the following for their assistance in the photography: Sunbeam Corporation Ltd; Kambrook; Maxwell & William; Home & Garden on the Mall; Verdi; Pillivuyut.

Fudge brownies, page 88

Spinach pie, page 84

Almond and pear pouches, page 104

All recipes are double-tested by our team of home economists. When we test our recipes, we rate them for ease of preparation. The following cookery ratings are on the recipes in this book, making them easy to use and understand.

A single Cooking with Confidence symbol indicates a recipe that is simple and generally quick to make —perfect for beginners.

Two symbols indicate the need for just a little more care and a little more time.

Three symbols indicate special dishes that need more investment in time, care and patience—but the results are worth it.

IMPORTANT
Those who might be at risk from the effects of salmonella food poisoning (the elderly, pregnant women, young children and those suffering from immune deficiency diseases) should consult their doctor with any concerns about eating raw eggs.

The low-down on low-fat

Eating low-fat isn't the same as being on a diet, but rather a change in eating habits that can stay with you for life, altering your tastes for good. Can't imagine a world without mayonnaise and cream? We'll show you how to 'adjust' some of your favourite recipes.

This isn't a diet book, but a cookbook of wholesome family meals with reduced fat— delicious alternatives to buying pre-packed supermarket low-fat dinners, many of which tend to be bland, insubstantial and quite expensive. What we've done is taken a selection of popular recipes and looked at reducing their fat content. We certainly haven't wanted to compromise on taste, so if your personal favourite isn't included, it may be because it tastes so great the way it is that a low-fat version would be a poor substitute. Luckily, our spaghetti bolognese, lasagne, potato wedges and even fudgy chocolate brownies all passed the low-fat taste test.

Fat is often portrayed as a villain and we must remember that it is not—everyone needs a certain amount of fat in their body, to help with growth and development and to carry fat-soluble vitamins throughout the body. It is the quantity and type of fat we eat that can cause problems. Foods contain a mix of different fats, but one type usually predominates.

Saturated fats, those that have been implicated in some health problems, are found mainly in animal products, including butter, cream, fat on meat and other fats which are solid at room temperature, like dripping or lard.

Mono-unsaturated fats, which are generally regarded as being better for us, are found in olives, olive oil, many vegetable oils, most nuts, avocados and, in small amounts, in fish,

chicken, lean meat and also eggs.

Polyunsaturated fats, found in nuts, grains, seeds and oily fish, usually remain soft or liquid at room temperature.

If you want to limit your fat intake, it is recommended you try to have no more than about 30–40 g of fat per day (30 g for women and small men, 40 g for men and taller women). With this in mind, we have carefully developed recipes that contain the following amounts of fat per serve:
• Soups with up to 8 g fat
• Mains with up to 15 g fat
• Desserts and baked ideas with up to 8 g fat.

Each recipe has the fat per serve clearly marked, so this will help you keep tabs on how much you are eating. For those who wish to change their dietary habits to eating low-fat but find it hard to accept the idea of giving up creamy sauces to eat plain 'undressed' vegetables or meat, we've come up with some special ideas that won't break the 'fat bank' (see pages 74–75).

If you are aiming to lose weight, cutting back on your fat intake is a good start and this book will certainly help you monitor that, but you also need to exercise regularly.

INGREDIENTS
As well as using the recipes in this book, once you get used to cooking and eating the low-fat way, you will find many of your favourite dishes don't need to be given up completely but can be adapted by using lower-fat ingredients. The tips on the previous page explain simple ways to change your cooking habits and other ways will become obvious when you try the recipes. For example, you can use low-fat natural yoghurt instead of sour cream, or whipped ricotta with orange (page 75) instead of whipped cream. When frying onions, use aerosol oil sprays and add a tablespoon of water to the pan to speed the softening process. Use fish canned in brine or spring water instead of oil.

These days we are lucky with the choice and variety of low-fat foods available—bread, dairy products including spreads and cheeses, and meat which is sold well trimmed and labelled according to its fat content. The lean pre-trimmed cuts are excellent—they mean you can't be tempted to leave the fat on in a weak moment. Some shop-bought mince has quite a high proportion of fat, so make your own from lean meat or choose the mince labelled low-fat. New Fashioned Pork and Trim Lamb are low-fat cuts of meat.

For cheeseaholics there are many fat-reduced Cheddars on the market but it is also worth knowing that other cheeses, such as fetta and ricotta, also have low-fat versions.

Read all the labels on food packaging. These will tell you how much fat is contained in a recommended serving size or in a 100 g portion. If there isn't a nutritional table on the packaging, the manufacturers must list the ingredients in order of the quantities used. If the fat is near the beginning of the ingredients, put it back and try another brand.

Be aware that just because a product is labelled 'light', this doesn't necessarily mean light in fat: it can mean low in salt, flavour, colour and weight or low in alcohol as in Light Beer. As well, don't be confused by foods claiming to be low-cholesterol or no-cholesterol—this doesn't necessarily mean low in fat—just low in animal fats. These foods, which may include nuts, nut products, margarines or oils, can still contain a high percentage of other fats. Processed foods tend to be higher in fat. The more natural and less prepared the food, the better it is for you.

LOW-FAT COOKING HINTS
In many of our recipes you will find 'cooking oil spray' in the ingredients list. This is readily available at supermarkets and is a great addition to the shopping trolley. It is simply oil under pressure in an aerosol: no chemicals are added. Sometimes lecithin, a natural preservative and emulsifier derived from egg yolks and legumes, is added to make the oil appear white so that you can see where you have already sprayed. We used it for greasing pans or coating food and found far less oil was needed, as it covers a larger area. For the low-fat cook, this is a must-have.

There are many ways of achieving low-fat results, using very little or no fat at all. Investing in a couple of non-stick saucepans and frying pans is a good start. They require only a quick spray with oil, if any, and then you can pan-fry knowing that nothing is going to stick. There's no need to keep pouring in extra oil.

Steaming is a very good alternative to roasting, as it locks in the natural flavours. Add herbs, spices or lemon juice to meat, chicken or fish, or drizzle with sauce, then wrap in foil or baking paper and seal securely to keep in all the flavours. Steam in a bamboo or metal steamer, open the parcels at the table and enjoy the aroma and flavour.

Stir-frying uses a minimal amount of oil to seal meat, and cooking is done quickly and at high temperatures so there is less opportunity for fat to be absorbed. The meat is then usually removed and set aside. When stir-frying vegetables, add a tablespoon of water to prevent them from sticking—this also produces steam which speeds up the cooking process even more. Return the meat to the pan, add any sauces and flavourings and toss well.

Grilling and barbecuing are not only low-fat but produce wonderful flavours. Lightly grease the grill or barbecue with oil spray or brush lightly with oil. If you grill on a rack, rather than a hotplate, fat can run off the meat and be discarded later.

DON'T GO HUNGRY

Snack on low-fat, high fibre and no-fat foods when the munchies hit:

● Fresh fruit and vegetables (but go easy on the avocado).
● Fresh fruit and vegetable juices.
● Skim milk and low-fat milk drinks; low-fat yoghurt.
● Pasta with tomato-based sauces.
● Steamed rice.
● Baked jacket potato with low-fat yoghurt and chives.
● Home-made muffins (see pages 98–99).
● Wholegrain bread and bread rolls; bagels; English muffins; crumpets with low-fat spread such as honey, jam or Vegemite.
● Some crispbreads (read the labels).
● Rice cakes.
● Plain popcorn and baked pretzels.
● Dried fruit.

SOUPS

CHICKEN CURRY LAKSA

Fat per serve: 8 g
Preparation time: 30 minutes
Total cooking time: 25 minutes
Serves 4

500 g (1 lb) chicken breast
    fillets
1 large onion, roughly chopped
5 cm (2 inch) piece ginger,
    chopped
8 cm (3 inch) piece galangal,
    peeled and chopped
1 stem lemon grass, white part
    only, roughly chopped
2 cloves garlic
1 fresh red chilli, seeded
    and chopped
2 teaspoons vegetable oil
2 tablespoons mild curry paste
2 cups (500 ml/16 fl oz) chicken
    stock
60 g (2 oz) rice vermicelli
50 g (1¾ oz) dried egg noodles
400 ml (13 fl oz) light coconut
    milk
10 snow peas, halved
3 spring onions, finely chopped
1 cup (90 g/3 oz) bean sprouts
½ cup (15 g/½ oz) fresh
    coriander leaves

1 Cut the chicken into bite-sized cubes. Process the onion, ginger, galangal, lemon grass, garlic and chilli in a food processor until finely chopped. Add the oil and process until the mixture has a paste-like consistency. Spoon into a large wok, add the curry paste and stir over low heat for 1–2 minutes, until aromatic. Take care not to burn.

2 Increase the heat to medium, add the chicken and stir for 2 minutes, or until the chicken is well coated. Stir in the chicken stock and mix well. Bring slowly to the boil, then simmer for 10 minutes, or until the chicken is cooked through.

3 Meanwhile, cut the vermicelli into shorter lengths using scissors. Cook the vermicelli and egg noodles separately in large pans of boiling water for 5 minutes each. Drain and rinse under cold water.

4 Just prior to serving, add the light coconut milk and snow peas to the chicken and heat through. To serve, divide the vermicelli and noodles among four warmed serving bowls. Pour the hot laksa over the top and garnish with the spring onion, bean sprouts and coriander leaves.

NUTRITION PER SERVE
Protein 30 g; Fat 8 g; Carbohydrate 4.5 g;
Dietary Fibre 3 g; Cholesterol 65 mg;
945 kJ (225 cal)

COOK'S FILE

Hint: If you prefer a more fiery laksa, use a medium or hot brand of paste or increase the amount of chillies.

Stir the curry paste into the onion mixture, over low heat, until aromatic.

Just before serving, stir the coconut milk into the chicken until heated.

SEAFOOD RAVIOLI IN GINGERY SOUP

Fat per serve: 7 g
Preparation time: 30 minutes
Total cooking time: 20 minutes
Serves 4

8 raw medium prawns
1 carrot, chopped
1 onion, chopped
1 celery stick, chopped
3 spring onions, thinly sliced
6 cm (2¹/2 inch) piece ginger,
   thinly shredded
1 tablespoon mirin
1 teaspoon kecap manis
1 tablespoon soy sauce
4 large scallops
100 g (3¹/2 oz) boneless white
   fish fillet
1 egg white
200 g (6¹/2 oz) round gow gee
   wrappers
¹/3 cup (10 g/¹/4 oz) small fresh
   coriander leaves

1 To make the soup, peel the prawns, reserve 4 for the ravioli filling and chop the rest into small pieces and reserve. Put the prawn heads and shells in a large pan, cook over high heat until starting to brown, then cover with 1 litre water. Add the carrot, onion and celery, bring to the boil, reduce the heat and simmer for 10 minutes. Strain and discard the prawn heads, shells and vegetables. Return the stock to a clean pan and add the spring onion, ginger, mirin, kecap manis and soy sauce. Set aside.
2 To make the ravioli, chop the whole reserved prawns with the scallops and fish in a food processor until smooth. Add enough egg white to bind. Lay half the gow gee wrappers on a work surface and place a rounded teaspoon of filling in the centre of each. Brush the edges with water. Top each with another wrapper and press the edges to seal, eliminating air bubbles as you go. Trim with a fluted cutter. Cover with plastic wrap.
3 Bring a large pan of water to the boil. Meanwhile, heat the stock and leave simmering. Just prior to serving, drop a few ravioli at a time into the boiling water. Cook for 2 minutes, remove with a slotted spoon and divide among heated bowls. Cook the chopped reserved prawns in the same water for 2 minutes; drain. Pour the hot stock over the ravioli and serve, sprinkled with the chopped cooked prawns and coriander leaves.

NUTRITION PER SERVE
Protein 17 g; Fat 7 g; Carbohydrate 65 g; Dietary Fibre 4.5 g; Cholesterol 125 mg; 1765 kJ (420 cal)

Stir the prawn heads and shells in a pan over high heat until lightly browned.

Brush the edge of one wrapper with water, then cover with another.

Cook each batch of ravioli for 2 minutes, then remove with a slotted spoon.

POTATO, BROCCOLI AND CORIANDER SOUP

Fat per serve: 0.5 g
Preparation time: 15 minutes
Total cooking time: 30 minutes
Serves 4–6

500 g (1 lb) broccoli
cooking oil spray
2 onions, finely chopped
2 cloves garlic, finely chopped
2 teaspoons ground cumin
1 teaspoon ground coriander
750 g (1¹/₂ lb) potatoes, cubed
2 small chicken stock cubes

1¹/₂ cups (375 ml/12 fl oz) skim milk
3 tablespoons finely chopped fresh coriander

1 Cut the broccoli into small pieces. Lightly spray the base of a large saucepan with cooking oil, then heat over medium heat and add the onion and garlic. Add 1 tablespoon water to prevent sticking. Cover and cook, stirring occasionally, over low heat for 5 minutes, or until the onion has softened and is lightly golden. Add the ground cumin and coriander and cook for 2 minutes.

2 Add the potato and broccoli to the pan, stir well and add the stock cubes and 1 litre of water. Slowly bring to the boil, reduce the heat, cover and simmer over low heat for 20 minutes, or until the vegetables are tender. Allow to cool slightly.

3 Blend the soup in batches in a food processor or blender until smooth. Return to the pan and stir in the milk. Slowly reheat, without boiling. Stir the chopped coriander through and season well with freshly cracked pepper and salt.

NUTRITION PER SERVE (6)
Protein 10 g; Fat 0.5 g; Carbohydrate 20 g; Dietary Fibre 6 g; Cholesterol 2 mg; 580 kJ (140 cal)

Chop all the broccoli into small, even-sized pieces.

Stir the ground cumin and coriander into the onion and cook for about 2 minutes.

Purée the mixture in batches, in a food processor or blender, until smooth.

LEEK AND POTATO SOUP

Fat per serve: 1 g
Preparation time: 20 minutes
Total cooking time: 40–45 minutes
Serves 4

cooking oil spray
2 leeks, white part only, sliced
3 cloves garlic, crushed
1 teaspoon ground cumin

1 kg (2 lb) potatoes, chopped
1.25 litres vegetable stock
1/2 cup (125 ml/4 fl oz) skim milk

1 Lightly spray a non-stick frying pan with oil. Add the leek and garlic, and 1 tablespoon water to prevent sticking, then cook over low heat, stirring frequently, for 25 minutes, or until the leek turns golden. Add the cumin and cook for 2 minutes.
2 Put the potato in a large pan with the leek mixture and stock, bring to the boil, reduce the heat and simmer for 10–15 minutes, or until the potato is tender. Cool a little, then purée in batches, in a processor or blender, until smooth. Return to the pan and season.
3 Stir in the milk and heat through before serving.

NUTRITION PER SERVE
Protein 8 g; Fat 1 g; Carbohydrate 35 g; Dietary Fibre 5.5 g; Cholesterol 1 mg; 795 kJ (190 cal)

Stir the leek and garlic over low heat for about 25 minutes, until golden.

Add the cooked leek mixture to the chopped potato and stock.

Purée the cooled mixture in batches in a food processor.

WON TON NOODLE SOUP

Fat per serve: 5 g
Preparation time: 25 minutes
Total cooking time: 25 minutes
Serves 4

70 g (2¼ oz) raw prawns
70 g (2¼ oz) veal mince
3 tablespoons soy sauce
1 tablespoon finely chopped
   spring onion
1 tablespoon finely chopped
   water chestnuts
1 teaspoon finely chopped ginger

2 cloves garlic, finely chopped
24 gow gee wrappers
1.25 litres chicken stock
2 tablespoons mirin
500 g (1 lb) baby bok choy,
   finely shredded
8 spring onions, sliced

1 Peel, devein and finely chop the prawns. Mix with the veal mince, 2 teaspoons soy sauce, spring onion, water chestnuts, ginger and garlic. Lay the round wrappers out on a work surface and place a teaspoon of mixture in the middle of each.
2 Moisten the edges of the wrappers

and bring up the sides to form a pouch. Pinch together to seal. Cook in batches in a large pan of rapidly boiling water for 4–5 minutes. Drain and divide among soup bowls.
3 Bring the stock, remaining soy sauce and mirin to the boil in a pan. Add the bok choy, cover and simmer for 2 minutes, or until the bok choy has just wilted. Add the sliced spring onion and season. Ladle the stock, bok choy and spring onion over the won tons.

NUTRITION PER SERVE
Protein 10 g; Fat 5 g; Carbohydrate 30 g; Dietary Fibre 5 g; Cholesterol 25 mg; 760 kJ (180 cal)

Peel the prawns and devein them before chopping them finely.

Bring the sides of the wrappers up around the filling and pinch to seal.

Add the finely shredded bok choy to the pan and simmer until just wilted.

PUMPKIN SOUP WITH CORIANDER PASTE

Fat per serve: 8 g
Preparation time: 20 minutes
Total cooking time: 40 minutes
Serves 6

2 teaspoons vegetable oil
2 teaspoons ground coriander
2 teaspoons ground cumin
1/2 teaspoon ground turmeric
1 onion, chopped
1 celery stick, chopped
1.5 kg (3 lb) pumpkin, chopped
2 1/2 cups (600 ml/20 fl oz)
   chicken stock

1 cup (250 ml/8 fl oz) light
   coconut milk

Coriander paste
1 cup (30g/1 oz) fresh coriander
   leaves
1/2 cup (10 g/1/4 oz) fresh mint
   leaves
1 tablespoon grated ginger
1 teaspoon caster sugar

1 Heat the oil in a large pan, add the spices and cook over low heat for 2 minutes, without browning. Add the onion, celery and pumpkin and stir for 2 minutes to coat the vegetables in the spice mixture. Add the stock and bring to the boil. Cover and simmer

for 30 minutes, or until the pumpkin is tender. Allow to cool slightly.
2 Purée the mixture in batches in a food processor until smooth. Return to the pan, stir in the coconut milk, season with salt and freshly ground black pepper and reheat gently. If too thick, stir in a little extra stock.
3 To make the coriander paste, finely chop the coriander and mint leaves. Combine in a bowl with the ginger and sugar. Spoon a little on top of the soup and stir through to add flavour, colour and texture.

NUTRITION PER SERVE
Protein 6 g; Fat 8 g; Carbohydrate 18 g;
Dietary Fibre 3.5 g; Cholesterol 0 mg;
1600 kJ (382 cal)

Stir the vegetables thoroughly until coated in the spices.

Let the mixture cool a little before puréeing, in case of splashes.

Mix the chopped coriander and mint with the ginger and sugar, to make the paste.

CHICKEN SOUP

Fat per serve: 5 g
Preparation time: 10 minutes
Total cooking time: 30 minutes
Serves 4

1 small leek, white part only
2 potatoes
2 chicken breast fillets
2 teaspoons oil

420 g (13 oz) can creamed corn
3 cups (750 ml/24 fl oz) chicken
   stock
1 tablespoon chopped fresh chives

1 Finely slice the leek, and chop the potatoes into cubes. Cut the chicken into very thin strips.
2 Heat the oil in a large pan, add the leek, cover and cook over low heat for 5 minutes, stirring occasionally, until very soft.

3 Add the potato, chicken, corn and stock to the leek in the pan. Stir to combine, bring to the boil, then reduce the heat and simmer for 20 minutes, or until the potato is very soft. Just before serving, garnish with the chives. Season with salt and freshly ground black pepper.

NUTRITION PER SERVE
Protein 30 g; Fat 5 g; Carbohydrate 25 g;
Dietary Fibre 5 g; Cholesterol 50 mg;
1110 kJ (265 cal)

Discard any excess fat from the chicken fillets and cut into small, thin strips.

Cook the sliced leek over low heat until it is very soft.

Add the potato, chicken, corn and stock and bring to the boil.

Pumpkin soup with coriander paste (top) and Chicken soup

MEDITERRANEAN FISH SOUP

Fat per serve: 7.5 g
Preparation time: 30 minutes
Total cooking time: 45 minutes
Serves 4

1/2 teaspoon saffron threads
3 teaspoons oil
2 large onions, thinly sliced
1 leek, white part only, chopped
4 cloves garlic, finely chopped
1 bay leaf, torn
1/2 teaspoon dried marjoram
1 teaspoon grated orange rind

2 tablespoons dry white wine
1 red capsicum, cut into chunks
500 g (1 lb) tomatoes, chopped
1/2 cup (125 ml/4 fl oz) tomato purée
2 cups (500 ml/16 fl oz) fish stock
2 tablespoons tomato paste
2 teaspoons soft brown sugar
500 g (1 lb) firm white fish, cut into bite-sized pieces
3 tablespoons chopped fresh parsley

1 Soak the saffron in 2 tablespoons boiling water; set aside. Heat the oil in a large heavy-based pan, over low heat. Add the onion, leek, garlic, bay leaf and marjoram. Cover and cook for 10 minutes, shaking the pan occasionally, until the onion is soft. Add the rind, wine, capsicum and tomato, cover and cook for 10 minutes.
2 Stir in the purée, stock, tomato paste, sugar and saffron (with liquid). Bring to the boil, reduce the heat and simmer, uncovered, for 15 minutes.
3 Add the fish to the soup, cover and cook for 8 minutes, or until tender. Add salt and pepper and half the parsley. Garnish with parsley.

NUTRITION PER SERVE
Protein 30 g; Fat 7.5 g; Carbohydrate 15 g;
Dietary Fibre 5 g; Cholesterol 90 mg;
1020 kJ (245 cal)

Soak the saffron threads in 2 tablespoons boiling water.

Add the orange rind, wine, capsicum and tomato, cover and cook for 10 minutes.

Add the fish pieces to the soup, cover and cook until tender.

VEGETABLE AND PASTA SOUP

Fat per serve: 2 g
Preparation time: 20 minutes
Total cooking time: 40 minutes
Serves 6

2 teaspoons olive oil
1 onion, chopped
1 carrot, chopped

2 celery sticks, chopped
350 g (11 oz) sweet potato,
  chopped
400 g (13 oz) can corn kernels,
  drained
1 litre vegetable stock
1 cup (90 g/3 oz) pasta spirals

1 Heat the oil in a large pan and add the onion, carrot and celery. Cook over low heat, stirring regularly, for 10 minutes, or until soft.

2 Add the sweet potato, corn kernels and stock. Bring to the boil, reduce the heat and simmer for 20 minutes, or until the vegetables are tender.

3 Add the pasta to the pan and return to the boil. Reduce the heat and simmer for 10 minutes, or until the pasta is tender. Serve immediately.

NUTRITION PER SERVE
Protein 4 g; Fat 2 g; Carbohydrate 25 g; Dietary Fibre 5 g; Cholesterol 0 mg; 555 kJ (135 cal)

Stir the onion, carrot and celery over low heat until soft.

Add the sweet potato, drained corn kernels and the stock.

When the vegetables are tender, add the pasta to the pan.

LEAN MEAT MAGIC

SHEPHERD'S PIE

Fat per serve: 7 g
Preparation time: 40 minutes
Total cooking time: 40 minutes
Serves 4

cooking oil spray
2 onions, thinly sliced
1 large carrot, finely chopped
2 celery sticks, finely chopped
500 g (1 lb) lean lamb mince
2 tablespoons plain flour
2 tablespoons tomato paste
2 tablespoons Worcestershire
   sauce
1 beef or chicken stock cube
1.25 kg (2¼ lb) potatoes
½ cup (125 ml/4 fl oz) skim milk
⅓ cup (20 g/¾ oz) finely
   chopped fresh parsley
paprika, to sprinkle

1 Lightly spray a large non-stick frying pan with oil, then heat. Add the onion, carrot and celery and stir constantly over medium heat for 5 minutes, until the vegetables begin to soften. Add 1 tablespoon water to prevent sticking. Remove from the pan and set aside. Spray the pan with a little more oil, add the lamb mince and cook over high heat until well browned.

2 Add the plain flour and stir for 2–3 minutes. Return the vegetables to the pan and add the tomato paste, Worcestershire sauce, stock cube and 2 cups (500 ml/16 fl oz) water. Stir and slowly bring to the boil. Reduce the heat, cover and simmer for 20 minutes, stirring occasionally to prevent sticking.

3 Meanwhile, chop the potatoes and cook until tender. Drain and mash until smooth. Add the milk, season with salt and freshly cracked pepper, then beat well.

4 Stir the chopped parsley through the mince and season well. Preheat a grill. Pour the mince into a 1.5 litre capacity baking dish. Spoon the potato over the top, spreading evenly with the back of the spoon. Use a fork to roughen up the potato and make the traditionally crunchy topping. Sprinkle lightly with paprika and grill until golden, watching carefully because the potato browns quickly.

NUTRITION PER SERVE
Protein 3 g; Fat 7 g; Carbohydrate 15 g; Dietary Fibre 2.5 g; Cholesterol 1 mg; 915 kJ (220 cal)

Add the tomato paste, Worcestershire sauce, stock cube and water.

Create a decorative effect by running the back of a fork across the potato.

BEEF AND VEGETABLE CASSEROLE

Fat per serve: 4 g
Preparation time: 40 minutes
Total cooking time: 1 hour 40 minutes
Serves 6

500 g (1 lb) lean round steak
cooking oil spray
1 onion, sliced
3 cloves garlic, crushed
2 teaspoons ground cumin
1 teaspoon dried thyme leaves
2 bay leaves
400 g (13 oz) can chopped
    tomatoes
500 g (1 lb) potatoes, chopped
2 large carrots, thickly sliced
4 zucchini, thickly sliced
250 g (8 oz) mushrooms, halved
250 g (8 oz) yellow squash,
    halved
2 tablespoons tomato paste
1/2 cup (125 ml/4 fl oz) red wine
1/3 cup (20 g/3/4 oz) chopped
    fresh parsley

1 Preheat the oven to moderate 180°C (350°F/Gas 4). Remove any excess fat and sinew from the meat and cut into 2 cm (3/4 inch) cubes. Spray a deep, non-stick frying pan with oil and fry the meat in batches until brown. Remove from the pan. Spray the pan again, add the onion and cook until lightly golden. Add the garlic, cumin, thyme and bay leaves; stir for 1 minute.
2 Return the meat and any juices to the pan, tossing to coat with spices. Add 1 1/2 cups (375 ml/12 fl oz) water and the tomato, scraping the pan. Simmer for 10 minutes, or until thickened. Mix in a large casserole dish with the vegetables, tomato paste and wine.

3 Bake, covered, for 1 hour. Stir well, then uncover and bake for 20 minutes. Season, remove the bay leaves and stir in the parsley.

NUTRITION PER SERVE
Protein 25 g; Fat 4 g; Carbohydrate 20 g; Dietary Fibre 6.5 g; Cholesterol 50 mg; 930 kJ (220 cal)

Discard any excess fat and sinew from the steak and cut the steak into cubes.

When the onion is golden, add the garlic, cumin, thyme and bay leaves.

Pour the wine into the casserole dish and stir through the vegetables.

TANDOORI LAMB SALAD

Fat per serve: 6.5 g
Preparation time: 20 minutes
  + overnight marinating
Total cooking time: 15 minutes
Serves 4

1 cup (250 g/8 oz) low-fat
  natural yoghurt
2 cloves garlic, crushed
2 teaspoons grated ginger
2 teaspoons ground turmeric
2 teaspoons garam masala

1/4 teaspoon paprika
2 teaspoons ground coriander
red food colouring, optional
500 g (1 lb) lean lamb fillets
4 tablespoons lemon juice
1 1/2 teaspoons chopped fresh
  coriander
1 teaspoon chopped fresh mint
150 g (5 oz) mixed salad leaves
1 large mango, cut into strips
2 cucumbers, cut into matchsticks

1 Mix the yoghurt, garlic, ginger and spices in a bowl, add a little colouring and toss with the lamb to thoroughly coat. Cover and refrigerate overnight.
2 Grill the lamb on a foil-lined baking tray under high heat for 7 minutes each side, or until the marinade starts to brown. Set aside for 5 minutes before serving.
3 Mix the lemon juice, coriander and mint, then season. Toss with the salad leaves, mango and cucumber, then arrange on plates. Slice the lamb and serve over the salad.

NUTRITION PER SERVE
Protein 30 g; Fat 6.5 g; Carbohydrate 8 g; Dietary Fibre 2 g; Cholesterol 90 mg; 965 kJ (230 cal)

Coat the lamb with the marinade, cover and refrigerate overnight.

Cut the mango flesh into long, thin strips, using a sharp knife.

Turn the lamb after about 7 minutes and cook until the marinade starts to brown.

MOUSSAKA

Fat per serve: 10 g
Preparation time: 30 minutes
Total cooking time: 1 hour 30 minutes
Serves 6

1 kg (2 lb) eggplants
cooking oil spray
400 g (13 oz) lean lamb mince
2 onions, finely chopped
2 cloves garlic, crushed
400 g (13 oz) can tomatoes
1 tablespoon chopped fresh thyme
1 teaspoon chopped fresh
    oregano
1 tablespoon tomato paste
1/3 cup (80 ml/2³/4 fl oz) dry
    white wine
1 bay leaf
1 teaspoon sugar

Cheese sauce
1¹/4 cups (315 ml/10 fl oz) skim
    milk
2 tablespoons plain flour
1/4 cup (30 g/1 oz) grated
    reduced-fat Cheddar
1 cup (250 g/8 oz) ricotta
pinch of cayenne pepper
1/4 teaspoon ground nutmeg

1 Cut the eggplant into 1 cm (1/2 inch) thick slices, place in a colander over a large bowl, layering with a generous sprinkling of salt, and leave to stand for 20 minutes. This is to draw out the bitter juices.
2 Lightly spray a non-stick frying pan with oil and brown the lamb mince, in batches if necessary, over medium-high heat. Once all the meat is browned, set aside.
3 Spray the pan again with oil, add the onion and stir continuously for 2 minutes. Add 1 tablespoon water to the pan to prevent sticking. Add the garlic and cook for about 3 minutes, or until the onion is golden brown.
4 Push the undrained tomatoes through a sieve, then discard the contents of the sieve.
5 Return the meat to the pan with the onion. Add the herbs, tomato pulp, tomato paste, wine, bay leaf and sugar. Cover and simmer over low heat for 20 minutes. Preheat a grill.
6 Thoroughly rinse and pat dry the eggplant, place on a grill tray, spray lightly with oil and grill under high heat until golden brown. Turn over, spray lightly with oil and grill until golden brown. Arrange half the eggplant slices over the base of a 1.5 litre capacity baking dish. Top with half the meat mixture and then repeat the layers.
7 Preheat the oven to moderate 180°C (350°F/Gas 4). To make the cheese sauce, blend a little of the milk with the flour to form a paste in a small pan. Gradually blend in the remaining milk, stirring constantly over low heat until the milk starts to simmer and thicken. Remove from the heat and stir in the Cheddar, ricotta, cayenne and nutmeg. Pour over the moussaka and bake for 35–40 minutes, or until the cheese is golden brown and the moussaka heated through.

NUTRITION PER SERVE
Protein 10 g; Fat 10 g; Carbohydrate 15 g; Dietary Fibre 5.5 g; Cholesterol 25 mg; 735 kJ (175 cal)

COOK'S FILE

Storage time: Freeze up to 2 months. Thaw in the fridge, then heat in a moderate oven for 30–45 minutes.

Sprinkle a generous amount of salt on the eggplant slices and set aside.

Empty the can of tomatoes into a sieve and push the tomatoes through.

Stir the herbs, tomato pulp, tomato paste, wine, bay leaf and sugar into the meat.

Rinse and dry the eggplant slices and grill on both sides until golden.

Layer the eggplant slices and meat evenly in the baking dish.

Remove from the heat before adding the Cheddar, ricotta, cayenne and nutmeg.

VEAL CUTLETS IN CHILLI TOMATO SAUCE

Fat per serve: 6 g
Preparation time: 35 minutes
Total cooking time: 35 minutes
Serves 4

5 slices wholemeal bread
3 tablespoons fresh parsley
3 cloves garlic
4 thick veal cutlets, trimmed
3 tablespoons skim milk
2 teaspoons olive oil
1 onion, finely chopped
1 tablespoon capers, drained
1 teaspoon canned green
    peppercorns, chopped
1 teaspoon chopped red chilli
2 tablespoons balsamic vinegar
1 teaspoon soft brown sugar
2 tablespoons tomato paste
440 g (14 oz) can chopped
    tomatoes

1 Preheat the oven to moderate 180°C (350°F/Gas 4). Place a rack in a small baking dish. Chop the bread, parsley and garlic in a food processor to make fine breadcrumbs.

2 Season the cutlets on both sides with salt and black pepper. Pour the milk into a bowl and put the breadcrumbs on a plate. Dip the veal in the milk, then coat in the crumbs, pressing the crumbs on. Transfer to the rack and bake for 20 minutes.

3 Meanwhile, heat the oil in a small pan over medium heat. Add the onion, capers, peppercorns and chilli, cover and cook for 8 minutes. Stir in the vinegar, sugar and tomato paste and stir until boiling. Stir in the tomato, reduce the heat and simmer for 15 minutes. Season, to taste.

4 Remove the cutlets from the rack and wipe the dish. Place about three-quarters of the tomato sauce in the base and put the cutlets on top. Spoon the remaining sauce over the cutlets and return to the oven. Reduce the oven to slow 150°C (300°F/Gas 2), then bake for another 10 minutes, or until heated through. Sprinkle with extra chopped parsley to garnish.

NUTRITION PER SERVE
Protein 15 g; Fat 6 g; Carbohydrate 20 g; Dietary Fibre 5 g; Cholesterol 25 mg; 845 kJ (200 cal)

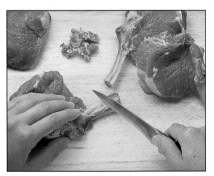

Trim the veal cutlets of any excess fat and gristle.

Dip the seasoned cutlets in the milk, then press into the breadcrumb mixture.

Put the cutlets on top of the tomato sauce, then top with the remaining sauce.

LINGUINE WITH BACON, MUSHROOMS AND PEAS

Fat per serve: 7 g
Preparation time: 20 minutes
Total cooking time: 25 minutes
Serves 4

3 bacon rashers
2 teaspoons olive oil
2–3 cloves garlic, crushed
1 red onion, chopped
185 g (6 oz) field mushrooms, sliced
1/3 cup (20 g/3/4 oz) chopped fresh parsley

1 cup (155 g/5 oz) peas
1 1/2 cups (375 ml/12 fl oz) low-fat light evaporated milk
2 teaspoons cornflour
325 g (11 oz) dried linguine
25 g (3/4 oz) Parmesan shavings

1 Remove the fat and rind from the bacon and chop roughly. Heat the oil in a medium pan, add the garlic, onion and bacon and cook over low heat for 5 minutes, stirring frequently, until the onion and bacon are soft. Add the sliced mushrooms and cook, stirring, for another 5 minutes, or until soft.
2 Add the parsley, peas and milk to the pan. Mix the cornflour with 1 tablespoon of water until smooth, add to the mixture and stir over medium heat until slightly thickened.
3 Meanwhile, put the pasta on to cook in a large pan of rapidly boiling, salted water for 8 minutes, or until *al dente*. Drain and serve with the hot sauce and Parmesan shavings.

NUTRITION PER SERVE
Protein 30 g; Fat 7 g; Carbohydrate 80 g; Dietary Fibre 9 g; Cholesterol 25 mg; 2085 kJ (500 cal)

COOK'S FILE

Note: Parmesan adds a nice flavour to this dish, but leave it out if you want to achieve a lower fat content.

Discard the fat and rind from the bacon and chop the meat roughly into strips.

When the onion is softened, add the sliced mushrooms and stir while cooking.

Stir the vegetable mixture until the liquid has slightly thickened.

FIGS WITH PROSCIUTTO AND GOATS CHEESE

Fat per serve: 9 g
Preparation time: 20 minutes
Total cooking time: 25 minutes
Makes 6

1–2 cloves garlic, crushed
1 tablespoon olive oil
6 slices baguette, cut on an angle
6 large fresh figs
6 thin slices prosciutto
80 g (2¾ oz) soft goats cheese
2 vine-ripened tomatoes, peeled, seeded and finely chopped

2 teaspoons olive oil
2 teaspoons balsamic vinegar
1 tablespoon chopped fresh chives

1 Preheat the oven to warm 160°C (315°F/Gas 2–3). Combine the garlic and oil in a small bowl and brush it lightly over both sides of the bread slices. Bake on a baking tray for 10 minutes, or until crisp and golden.
2 Meanwhile, cut a 2.5 cm (1 inch) deep cross into the top of each fig. Wrap each fig loosely in foil and seal. Place upright on a baking tray and bake for about 10–12 minutes, until warmed through.

3 Open the foil and carefully wrap each warm fig in a slice of prosciutto. Place some goats cheese over the top of each fig. Return, uncovered, to the oven for 3–4 minutes, until the goats cheese is warmed through.
4 To serve, divide the tomato among serving plates, drizzle with the olive oil and balsamic vinegar and sprinkle with the chopped fresh chives. Place a fig in the centre of each plate and serve at once with the bread slices.

NUTRITION PER SERVE
Protein 9 g; Fat 9 g; Carbohydrate 20 g; Dietary Fibre 2.5 g; Cholesterol 10 mg; 835 kJ (200 cal)

Brush the oil and garlic mixture over the slices of bread and bake until golden.

Cut a deep cross into the top of each fig and wrap individually in foil.

Wrap prosciutto around each fig and put goats cheese on top.

PENNE WITH RICOTTA AND BASIL SAUCE

Fat per serve: 10 g
Preparation time: 20 minutes
Total cooking time:15 minutes
Serves 4

2 teaspoons olive oil
2 rashers bacon, chopped, rind and fat removed
2–3 cloves garlic, crushed
1 onion, finely chopped
2 spring onions, finely chopped
250 g (8 oz) ricotta
1/2 cup (30 g/1 oz) finely chopped fresh basil
325 g (11 oz) penne
8 cherry tomatoes, halved

1 Heat the oil in a pan, add the bacon, garlic, onion and spring onion and stir over medium heat for 5 minutes, or until cooked. Remove from the heat, stir in the ricotta and chopped basil and beat until smooth.

2 Meanwhile, cook the pasta in a large pan of rapidly boiling salted water for 10 minutes, or until *al dente*. Just prior to draining the pasta, add about a cup of the pasta water to the ricotta mixture to thin the sauce. Add more water if you prefer an even thinner sauce. Season well.

3 Drain the pasta and stir the sauce through with the tomato halves. Can be garnished with small basil leaves.

NUTRITION PER SERVE
Protein 20 g; Fat 10 g; Carbohydrate 65 g; Dietary Fibre 5 g; Cholesterol 40 mg; 1885 kJ (450 cal)

Remove from the heat and stir in the ricotta and chopped basil.

Bring a large pan of salted water to a rapid boil before adding the pasta.

Thin the ricotta mixture with about a cup of the water from the cooked pasta.

Salads

Refreshing salads can be satisfying as a light meal in themselves, but are
also a welcome side dish to many of the low-fat meals in this book.

TOMATO AND BASIL

Quarter 6 ripe Roma tomatoes and
combine with 1 finely sliced red onion,
1 crushed garlic clove, 1 cup (60 g/
2 oz) finely shredded basil leaves and
1–2 tablespoons balsamic vinegar.
Toss. Season, set aside for 10 minutes,
then transfer to a shallow dish. If you
find onion too strong, put it in a bowl
and cover with boiling water for
5 minutes. Drain well. Serves 4.

NUTRITION PER SERVE
Protein 2 g; Fat 0 g; Carbohydrate 5 g;
Dietary Fibre 2 g; Cholesterol 0 mg;
120 kJ (30 cal)

HOT BEANS WITH YOGHURT

Combine 100 g (3½ oz) each of dried
chickpeas, pinto beans, red kidney
beans and black-eyed beans in a large,
bowl. Cover with water and soak
overnight. Drain, place in a large pan
and cover with water. Bring to the
boil, reduce the heat and simmer for
45 minutes, or until tender. Don't
overcook or they will be mushy.
Meanwhile, in a large, deep non-stick
frying pan, cook 2 sliced onions over
low heat for 25 minutes, or until
golden. Add 2 teaspoons ground cumin
and 1 teaspoon ground coriander with
the beans; toss. Add a 420 g (13 oz)
can drained corn kernels, 2 chopped
tomatoes, ¹/3 cup (80 ml/2³/4 fl oz)
lemon juice and ¹/4 cup (7 g/¹/4 oz)
chopped coriander leaves. Season and
stir. Grate a Lebanese cucumber and,
with your hands, squeeze out the
moisture. Combine with 1 cup (250 g/
8 oz) low-fat natural yoghurt. Season,
then stir. Put the hot beans on a serving
plate. Top with yoghurt mix. Serves 8.

NUTRITION PER SERVE
Protein 10 g; Fat 2 g; Carbohydrate 25 g;
Dietary Fibre 8.5 g; Cholesterol 1.5 mg;
745 kJ (180 cal)

Clockwise, from top left: Grilled vegetables; Hot beans with yoghurt; Rocket and citrus with honey dressing; Roast pumpkin and onion with rocket; Tomato and basil.

ROAST PUMPKIN AND ONION WITH ROCKET

Preheat the oven to moderately hot 200°C (400°F/Gas 6). Cut 800 g (1 lb 10 oz) peeled jap pumpkin into 3 cm (1¼ inch) cubes and 2 small red onions into small wedges. Line a small baking dish with baking paper, add the vegetables and sprinkle with 2 finely chopped garlic cloves. Lightly spray with oil. Season and cook for 30–35 minutes, or until the pumpkin is just tender. Set aside. Tear the leaves from 150 g (5 oz) rocket into pieces. Arrange on a platter, then top with the pumpkin and onion. Drizzle all over with 1–2 tablespoons balsamic vinegar. Serve warm. Serves 4.

NUTRITION PER SERVE
Protein 5.5 g; Fat 1 g; Carbohydrate 15 g; Dietary Fibre 4 g; Cholesterol 0 mg; 400 kJ (95 cal)

GRILLED VEGETABLES

Mix 1.5 kg (3 lb) of thickly sliced vegetables (such as pumpkin, potato, parsnip, eggplant and zucchini) with 2 tablespoons olive oil and 4 finely chopped cloves garlic in a large baking dish. Heat a large flat grill or barbecue plate and spray lightly with cooking oil. Grill the vegetables separately (they will cook at different rates), turning until charred. Bake for 15 minutes on a lightly greased baking tray in a moderate (180°C (350°F/Gas 4) oven until cooked. Arrange 300 g (10 oz) baby spinach leaves on a platter, top with the vegetables and half a thinly sliced red capsicum. Drizzle with 2 tablespoons balsamic vinegar and chopped chives. Serves 4.

NUTRITION PER SERVE
Protein 9 g; Fat 10 g; Carbohydrate 25 g; Dietary Fibre 10 g; Cholesterol 0 mg; 1000 kJ (240 cal)

ROCKET AND CITRUS WITH HONEY DRESSING

Remove the rind from 1 grapefruit, 2 small red grapefruit and 4 oranges. Remove and discard all the pith from a few slices of the rind from each fruit and cut the rind into long thin strips. Remove any remaining pith from the fruit and slice between each section. Segment the fruits over a bowl to catch any juice; set the juice aside. Put the segments and rind in a salad bowl with 1 sliced red onion and ⅓ cup (10 g/¼ oz) fresh coriander leaves. Add 2 tablespoons honey and ⅓ cup (80 ml/2¾ fl oz) raspberry vinegar to the reserved fruit juice and whisk to combine. Pour over the salad and toss. Serve on a bed of rocket. Serves 6.

NUTRITION PER SERVE
Protein 3 g; Fat 0 g; Carbohydrate 25 g; Dietary Fibre 3.5 g; Cholesterol 0 mg; 505 kJ (120 cal)

PORK, BEER AND CHICKPEA STEW

Fat per serve: 10 g
Preparation time: 35 minutes
Total cooking time: 1 hour 30 minutes
Serves 4

2 teaspoons ground cumin
1 teaspoon ground coriander
1/2 teaspoon chilli powder
1/4 teaspoon ground cinnamon
400 g (13 oz) lean diced pork, trimmed
1 tablespoon plain flour
1 tablespoon olive oil
1 large onion, finely chopped
3 cloves garlic, finely chopped
2 large carrots, chopped
2 celery sticks, sliced
1/2 cup (125 ml/4 fl oz) chicken stock
1/2 cup (125 ml/4 fl oz) beer
2 ripe tomatoes, chopped
310 g (10 oz) can chickpeas, rinsed
2 tablespoons chopped fresh parsley

1 Cook the spices in a dry frying pan over low heat, shaking the pan, for 1 minute, or until aromatic.
2 Combine the pork, trimmed of all fat, with the spices and flour in a plastic bag and toss well. Remove the pork and shake off excess flour. Heat the oil in a large heavy-based pan over high heat and cook the pork, tossing regularly, for 8 minutes, or until lightly browned.
3 Add the onion, garlic, carrot, celery and half the stock to the pan and toss well. Cover and cook for 10 minutes. Add the remaining stock, beer and tomato and season with salt and pepper, to taste. Bring to the boil, reduce the heat, cover with a tight-fitting lid, then simmer over low heat for 1 hour. Gently shake the pan occasionally, but do not remove the lid during cooking. Stir in the chickpeas and fresh parsley. Simmer, uncovered, for 5 minutes and serve.

NUTRITION PER SERVE
Protein 40 g; Fat 10 g; Carbohydrate 35 g; Dietary Fibre 15 g; Cholesterol 50 mg; 1720 kJ (410 cal)

Chop the carrots into quite small pieces and thinly slice the celery sticks.

Dry-fry the spices over low heat, stirring the spices and shaking the pan.

Cook the flour-coated pork, tossing regularly, until lightly browned.

BEEF STROGANOFF

Fat per serve: 4 g
Preparation time: 20 minutes
Total cooking time: 25 minutes
Serves 4

500 g (1 lb) rump steak
cooking oil spray
1 onion, sliced
1/4 teaspoon paprika
250 g (8 oz) button mushrooms,
    halved

2 tablespoons tomato paste
1/2 cup (125 ml/4 fl oz) beef stock
1/2 cup (125 ml/4 fl oz) low-fat
    light evaporated milk
3 teaspoons cornflour
chopped fresh parsley, for serving

1 Remove any excess fat from the steak and slice into thin strips. Cook in batches in a large, lightly greased non-stick frying pan over high heat, until just cooked. Remove from the pan.
2 Lightly spray the pan and cook the onion, paprika and mushrooms over medium heat until the onion has softened. Add the meat, tomato paste, stock and 1/2 cup (125 ml/4 fl oz) water. Bring to the boil, then reduce the heat and simmer for 10 minutes.
3 In a small bowl, mix the evaporated milk with the cornflour. Add to the pan and stir until the sauce boils and thickens. Season well and sprinkle with parsley. Delicious over pasta.

NUTRITION PER SERVE
Protein 35 g; Fat 4 g; Carbohydrate 8 g;
Dietary Fibre 2.5 g; Cholesterol 85 mg;
900 kJ (215 cal)

Slice the rump steak into thin strips after removing any excess fat.

Stir the onion, paprika and mushrooms until the onion has softened.

Stir the evaporated milk into the cornflour until the mixture is smooth.

MEATLOAF

Fat per serve: 9 g
Preparation time: 15 minutes
Total cooking time: 1 hour 20 minutes
Serves 6

cooking oil spray
2 onions, finely chopped
2 cloves garlic, crushed
1½ cups (120 g/4 oz) fresh
  breadcrumbs
60 g (2 oz) pumpkin, coarsely
  grated
1 carrot, coarsely grated
2 tablespoons chopped fresh
  parsley
500 g (1 lb) extra-lean beef mince
2 tablespoons Worcestershire
  sauce
1 teaspoon dried basil
1 tablespoon tomato paste
1 egg, lightly beaten
90 g (3 oz) button mushrooms,
  thinly sliced

Tomato sauce
400 g (13 oz) can tomatoes
1 tablespoon dry white wine
2 teaspoons soft brown sugar

1 Preheat the oven to moderately hot 200°C (400°F/Gas 6). Lightly spray a non-stick frying pan with oil, heat and cook the onion, stirring, for 2 minutes. Add 1 tablespoon water to prevent sticking, then add the crushed garlic and stir for 3 minutes, or until the onion is golden brown. Allow to cool.
2 Use your hands to thoroughly mix together the breadcrumbs, pumpkin, carrot, parsley, mince, Worcestershire sauce, basil, tomato paste and the cooled onion mixture. Mix in the egg and mushrooms. Season. Transfer to a

10 x 18 cm (4 x 7 inch) non-stick loaf tin (or loaf tin lined with greaseproof paper), pressing gently into the tin and smoothing the top.
3 To make the tomato sauce, push the undrained tomatoes through a sieve, discarding the contents of the sieve. Stir in the wine and sugar. Spoon 3 tablespoons over the meatloaf and bake for 15 minutes.

Spoon another 3 tablespoons of sauce over the meatloaf, lower the oven temperature to 190°C (375°F/Gas 5) and bake for 1 hour 10 minutes, basting occasionally with sauce. Slice and serve with any remaining sauce.

NUTRITION PER SERVE
Protein 7 g; Fat 9 g; Carbohydrate 25 g; Dietary Fibre 4 g; Cholesterol 30 mg; 615 kJ (150 cal)

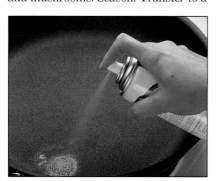

Lightly cover the base of the pan with cooking oil spray.

Using your hands is the easiest way to combine the ingredients.

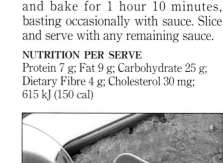

Spoon 3 tablespoons of the tomato sauce over the meatloaf.

PESTO BEEF SALAD

Fat per serve: 10 g
Preparation time: 30 minutes
Total cooking time: 25 minutes
Serves 4

100 g (3¹/2 oz) button mushrooms
1 large yellow capsicum
1 large red capsicum
cooking oil spray
100 g (3¹/2 oz) lean fillet steak
1¹/2 cups (135 g/4¹/2 oz) penne

Pesto
1 cup (50 g/1³/4 oz) fresh basil
    leaves, tightly packed

2 cloves garlic, chopped
2 tablespoons pepitas
    (pumpkin seeds)
1 tablespoon olive oil
2 tablespoons orange juice
1 tablespoon lemon juice

1 Cut the mushrooms into quarters. Cut the capsicums into quarters, discarding the seeds and membrane. Grill the capsicum, skin-side-up, until the skins blacken and blister. Cool under a damp tea towel, then peel and dice the flesh.

2 Spray a non-stick frying pan with oil and cook the steak over high heat for 3–4 minutes each side. Remove and leave for 5 minutes before cutting into thin slices. Season with a little salt.

3 To make the pesto, finely chop the basil leaves, garlic and pepitas in a food processor. With the motor running, add the oil, lemon and orange juice. Season with salt and pepper.

4 Meanwhile, cook the penne in a large pan of rapidly boiling salted water until *al dente*. Drain, then toss with the pesto in a large bowl.

5 Add the capsicum pieces, steak slices and mushroom quarters to the penne and toss to distribute evenly. Serve immediately.

NUTRITION PER SERVE
Protein 15 g; Fat 10 g; Carbohydrate 30 g; Dietary Fibre 4 g; Cholesterol 15 mg; 1330 kJ (270 cal)

When the capsicum has cooled, peel and dice the flesh.

Cook the steak in a non-stick frying pan until medium-rare.

Add the oil as well as the orange and lemon juice, in a thin stream.

PORK ROLLS WITH ROASTED CAPSICUM

Fat per serve: 5 g
Preparation time: 40 minutes
Total cooking time: 30 minutes
Serves 4

Sauce
3/4 cup (185 ml/6 fl oz) beef
    stock
2 teaspoons soy sauce
2 tablespoons red wine
2 teaspoons wholegrain mustard
2 teaspoons cornflour

1 red capsicum
4 x 150 g (5 oz) lean pork leg
    steaks
1/3 cup (90 g/3 oz) ricotta
2 spring onions, finely chopped
1 clove garlic, crushed
75 g (2 1/2 oz) rocket
4 small lean slices prosciutto
    (about 35 g/1 1/4 oz)
cooking oil spray

1 To make the sauce, put the beef stock, soy sauce, red wine and mustard in a pan. Blend the cornflour with 1 tablespoon water and add to the pan. Stir until the mixture boils and thickens.

2 Cut the capsicum into quarters and remove the seeds and membrane. Grill until the skin blisters and blackens. Cool under a damp tea towel, peel and cut the flesh into thin strips.

3 Flatten each steak into a thin square between 2 sheets of plastic, using a rolling pin or mallet. Combine the ricotta, onion and garlic in a bowl, then spread evenly over the pork. Top with a layer of rocket and prosciutto. Place a quarter of the capsicum at one end and roll up to enclose the capsicum. Tie with string or secure with toothpicks at even intervals.

4 Lightly spray a non-stick pan with oil and fry the pork rolls over medium heat for 5 minutes, or until well browned all over. Add the sauce to the pan and simmer over low heat for 10–15 minutes, or until the rolls are cooked through. Remove the string or toothpicks. Slice and serve with the sauce.

NUTRITION PER SERVE
Protein 40 g; Fat 5 g; Carbohydrate 3.5 g; Dietary Fibre 1 g; Cholesterol 95 mg; 925 kJ (220 cal)

Flatten the pork between two pieces of plastic wrap, using a rolling pin or mallet.

Secure the pork rolls with string or toothpicks at even intervals.

Add the sauce to the pan and simmer over low heat until cooked through.

PORK, BOK CHOY AND BLACK BEAN STIR-FRY

Fat per serve: 3 g
Preparation time: 20 minutes
Total cooking time: 10 minutes
Serves 4

400 g (13 oz) lean pork leg steaks
1 tablespoon canned salted black
  beans, rinsed
500 g (1 lb) baby bok choy
2 teaspoons sesame oil
2 onions, finely sliced
2 cloves garlic, finely chopped

2–3 teaspoons chopped ginger
1 red capsicum, cut into strips
1/2 cup (90 g/3 oz) water
  chestnuts, finely sliced
2 tablespoons oyster sauce
1 tablespoon soy sauce
2 teaspoons fish sauce

1 Slice the pork steaks into strips, cutting across the grain. Roughly chop the beans. Cut the ends off the bok choy, separate the leaves and shred.
2 Heat half the sesame oil in a large non-stick frying pan or wok. Cook the onion, garlic and ginger over high heat for 3–4 minutes, add the

capsicum and cook for 2–3 minutes. Remove from the pan. Heat the remaining sesame oil and stir-fry the pork in batches over high heat.
3 Return all the pork to the pan along with the onion mixture, black beans, shredded bok choy, water chestnuts and oyster, soy and fish sauces. Toss quickly to combine the ingredients, lower the heat and cover and steam for 3–4 minutes, or until the bok choy has just wilted. Serve immediately.

NUTRITION PER SERVE
Protein 30 g; Fat 3 g; Carbohydrate 20 g;
Dietary Fibre 3.5 g; Cholesterol 55 mg;
910 kJ (215 cal)

Shred the trimmed bok choy after separating the leaves.

Stir-fry the pork strips in batches over high heat until brown.

Toss all the ingredients quickly until combined, then lower the heat.

LASAGNE

Fat per serve: 12 g
Preparation time: 40 minutes
Total cooking time: 1 hour 35 minutes
Serves 8

2 teaspoons olive oil
1 large onion, chopped
2 carrots, finely chopped
2 celery sticks, finely chopped
2 zucchini, finely chopped
2 cloves garlic, crushed
500 g (1 lb) lean beef mince
2 x 400 g (13 oz) cans crushed
　　tomatoes
1/2 cup (125 ml/4 fl oz) beef
　　stock
2 tablespoons tomato paste
2 teaspoons dried oregano
375 g (12 oz) instant or fresh
　　lasagne sheets

Cheese sauce
1/3 cup (40 g/1 1/4 oz) cornflour
3 cups (750 ml/24 fl oz) skim
　　milk
100 g (3 1/2 oz) reduced-fat
　　cheese, grated

1 Heat the olive oil in a large non-stick frying pan. Add the onion and cook for 5 minutes, until soft. Add the carrot, celery and zucchini and cook, stirring constantly, for 5 minutes, or until the vegetables are soft. Add the crushed garlic and cook for another minute. Add the beef mince and cook over high heat, stirring, until well browned. Break up any lumps of meat with a wooden spoon.
2 Add the crushed tomato, beef stock, tomato paste and dried oregano to the pan and stir to thoroughly combine. Bring the mixture to the boil, then reduce the heat and simmer gently, partially covered, for 20 minutes, stirring occasionally to prevent the mixture sticking to the pan.
3 Preheat the oven to moderate 180°C (350°F/Gas 4). Spread a little of the meat sauce into the base of a 23 x 30 cm (9 x 12 inch) ovenproof dish. Arrange a layer of lasagne sheets in the dish, breaking some of the sheets, if necessary, to fit in neatly.
4 Spread half the meat sauce over the top to cover evenly. Cover with another layer of lasagne sheets, a layer of meat sauce, then a final layer of lasagne sheets.
5 To make the cheese sauce, blend a little of the milk with the cornflour, to form a smooth paste, in a small pan. Gradually blend in the remaining milk and stir constantly over low heat until the mixture boils and thickens. Remove from the heat and stir in the grated cheese until melted. Spread evenly over the top of the lasagne and bake for 1 hour.
6 Check the lasagne after 25 minutes. If the top is browning too quickly, cover loosely with non-stick baking paper or foil. Take care when removing the baking paper or foil that the topping does not come away with the paper. For serving, cut the lasagne into eight portions and garnish with fresh herbs.

NUTRITION PER SERVE
Protein 15 g; Fat 12 g; Carbohydrate 50 g; Dietary Fibre 5 g; Cholesterol 10 mg; 1885 kJ (450 cal)

COOK'S FILE
Storage time: Can be frozen for up to 2–3 months. When required, thaw overnight in the refrigerator, then reheat, covered with foil, for about 30 minutes in a moderate oven.

Chop the garlic and crush using the flat side of a large knife.

Add the vegetables to the pan and stir constantly until soft.

When you add the meat, break up any lumps with a wooden spoon.

Spread a little of the meat sauce over the base and cover evenly with lasagne sheets.

Remove the pan from the heat and stir in the cheese until melted.

Spread the cheese sauce evenly over the top of the lasagne.

BEEF AND VEGETABLE CURRY

Fat per serve: 8.5 g
Preparation time: 30 minutes
Total cooking time: 2 hours 30 minutes
Serves 4

2 teaspoons oil
1 large onion, chopped
2 cloves garlic, crushed
1 tablespoon grated ginger
2 teaspoons chopped fresh
    red chilli
2 teaspoons ground cumin
2 teaspoons ground coriander
1 teaspoon ground cardamom
1 teaspoon ground turmeric
½ teaspoon ground cloves
750 g (1 lb 8 oz) lean beef, cubed
400 g (13 oz) can crushed
    tomatoes
1 cup (250 ml/8 fl oz) beef stock
650 g (1 lb 5 oz) potatoes, cut
    into large chunks
125 g (4 oz) green beans, sliced
2 carrots, sliced
½ cup (125 ml/4 fl oz) low-fat
    natural yoghurt

1 Heat the oil in a large pan, add the onion and cook over low heat for 15 minutes, stirring regularly, until soft. Add the garlic, ginger, chilli and spices and stir for 1 minute.

2 Add the beef and stir to coat with the spices. Add the tomato and beef stock and bring to the boil. Reduce the heat to very low, cover and simmer for 1½ hours.

3 Add the potato, cook for 25 minutes, then uncover, add the beans and carrots and cook for 15 minutes, or until the vegetables are tender and the sauce thickens. Stir in the yoghurt, heat through and serve.

NUTRITION PER SERVE
Protein 45 g; Fat 8.5 g; Carbohydrate 30 g; Dietary Fibre 6.5 g; Cholesterol 125 mg; 1660 kJ (395 cal)

Stir the onion over low heat until soft and golden.

Stir the beef until coated thoroughly with the spices.

Add the chopped potato, cover and cook for 25 minutes.

LAMB CUTLETS WITH CANNELLINI PUREE

Fat per serve: 8 g
Preparation time: 30 minutes
  + 1 hour refrigeration
Total cooking time: 20 minutes
Serves 4

8 lamb cutlets
1 tablespoon fresh rosemary,
    roughly chopped
4 cloves garlic
2 teaspoons olive oil
2 x 400 g (13 oz) cans
    cannellini beans, drained

1 teaspoon ground cumin
1/2 cup (125 ml/4 fl oz) lemon
    juice
cooking oil spray
2 tablespoons balsamic vinegar

1 Trim the cutlets of excess fat from the outside edge and scrape the fat away from the bones. Place in a single layer in a shallow dish. Thinly slice 2 garlic cloves and mix with the rosemary, oil and 1/2 teaspoon salt and cracked black pepper. Pour over the meat, cover and refrigerate for 1 hour.
2 Rinse the cannellini beans and purée with the remaining garlic, the cumin and half the lemon juice in a food processor. Transfer to a pan, then set aside.
3 Lightly spray a non-stick frying pan with oil and cook the cutlets over medium heat for 1–2 minutes on each side. Add the vinegar and cook for 1 minute, turning to coat. Remove the cutlets and cover to keep warm. Add the remaining lemon juice to the pan and simmer for 2–3 minutes, or until the sauce thickens slightly. Warm the purée over medium heat and serve with the cutlets.

NUTRITION PER SERVE
Protein 30 g; Fat 8 g; Carbohydrate 45 g; Dietary Fibre 3.5 g; Cholesterol 50 mg; 1560 kJ (375 cal)

Peel 2 of the garlic cloves and thinly slice with a sharp knife.

Trim all the excess fat from the cutlets, scraping any away from the bones.

After cooking the cutlets lightly on each side, add the vinegar to the pan.

HUNGARIAN STYLE PORK AND LENTIL STEW

Fat per serve: 8 g
Preparation time: 20 minutes
Total cooking time: 1 hour
Serves 4

1 tablespoon olive oil
2 onions, chopped
500 g (1 lb) lean diced pork
2 teaspoons sweet Hungarian
  paprika
1 teaspoon hot paprika
½ teaspoon dried thyme

2 tablespoons tomato paste
2 teaspoons soft brown sugar
¼ cup (60 g/2 oz) red lentils
1½ cups (375 ml/12 fl oz) beef
  stock
1 tomato, to garnish
2 tablespoons low-fat natural
  yoghurt

1 Heat the olive oil in a large, deep saucepan over high heat. Add the onion, pork and paprika and stir for 3–4 minutes, until browned.
2 Add the thyme, tomato paste, sugar, lentils, stock and salt and freshly ground black pepper. Bring to

the boil, reduce the heat to very low and cook, covered, for 20 minutes, stirring occasionally to prevent sticking. Uncover and cook for another 15–20 minutes, or until thickened.
3 Remove from the heat and set aside for 10 minutes. To prepare the tomato, cut in half and scoop out the seeds. Slice the flesh into thin strips.
4 Just before serving, stir the yoghurt into the stew. Scatter with tomato. Can be served with rice.

NUTRITION PER SERVE
Protein 35 g; Fat 8 g; Carbohydrate 13 g;
Dietary Fibre 4 g; Cholesterol 70 mg;
1110 kJ (265 cal)

Stir the onion, pork and paprika until the pork is browned on all sides.

Add the beef stock to the pan and bring to the boil.

To make the tomato garnish, remove the seeds and slice the flesh into thin strips.

SPAGHETTI BOLOGNESE

Fat per serve: 8 g
Preparation time: 30 minutes
Total cooking time: 1 hour 20 minutes
Serves 4–6

cooking oil spray
2 onions, finely chopped
2 cloves garlic, finely chopped
2 carrots, finely chopped
2 celery sticks, finely chopped
400 g (13 oz) lean beef mince
1 kg (2 1b) tomatoes, chopped
1/2 cup (125 ml/4 fl oz) red wine

350 g (11 oz) spaghetti
1/4 cup (15 g/1/2 oz) finely
    chopped fresh parsley

1 Lightly spray a large saucepan with oil. Heat over medium heat, add the onion, garlic, carrot and celery. Stir over medium heat for 5 minutes, or until the vegetables have softened. If you find the vegetables are sticking, add 1 tablespoon water.
2 Increase the heat to high, add the mince and cook for 5 minutes, or until browned. Stir constantly to prevent the meat sticking. Add the tomato, wine and 1 cup (250 ml/8 fl oz) water.

Bring to the boil, reduce the heat and simmer, uncovered, for about 1 hour, until the sauce has thickened.
3 Cook the spaghetti in a large pan of rapidly boiling salted water for 10–12 minutes, or until *al dente*. Drain, stir the parsley through the sauce and season well with freshly cracked pepper and salt. Divide the spaghetti among pasta bowls and top with the bolognese sauce. Garnish with a little chopped fresh parsley.

NUTRITION PER SERVE (6)
Protein 9 g; Fat 8 g; Carbohydrate 50 g;
Dietary Fibre 7 g; Cholesterol 0 mg;
1695 kJ (405 cal)

Finely chop both the onions and then fry with the garlic, carrot and celery.

Stir the meat constantly and break up any lumps with the back of the spoon.

Simmer the bolognese sauce until the sauce has thickened.

MEATBALLS IN TOMATO SAUCE

Fat per serve: 8 g
Preparation time: 40 minutes
Total cooking time: 1 hour 45 minutes
Serves 6

500 g (1 lb) lean veal mince
1 onion, very finely chopped
4 cloves garlic, finely chopped
1 egg white, lightly beaten
1 cup (80 g/2³/4 oz) fresh white
    breadcrumbs
¹/2 cup (30 g/1 oz) finely
    chopped fresh parsley
3 tablespoons finely chopped
    fresh oregano
cooking oil spray
1.5 kg (3 lb) ripe tomatoes
2 onions, finely sliced
¹/2 cup (125 g/4 oz) tomato paste
¹/2 teaspoon sugar
350 g (12 oz) penne

1 Combine the veal mince, onion, half the garlic, the egg white, breadcrumbs, two-thirds of the parsley and 1 tablespoon of the oregano in a large bowl. Season well with salt and freshly cracked pepper. Mix with your hands until well combined. Shape into small balls (approximately 36). Spray a large non-stick frying pan with oil. Cook a third of the meatballs over high heat for 4–5 minutes, or until browned, turning constantly to prevent the meatballs sticking. Remove from the pan and repeat with the remaining meatballs, using a minimum of oil.
2 Score a cross in the base of each tomato, place in a heatproof bowl and cover with boiling water. Leave for 1 minute, or until the skins start to

come away. Drain, plunge into a bowl of iced water, then peel the skin away from the cross and roughly chop the flesh.
3 Lightly spray the base of a large, deep non-stick saucepan. Add the sliced onion and remaining garlic and cook over low heat for 2–3 minutes, stirring constantly. Add 2 tablespoons water, cover and cook gently for 5 minutes to soften the onion. Stir in the tomato and tomato paste. Cover and simmer for 10 minutes, uncover and simmer gently for 40 minutes.

Add the meatballs, cover and simmer for another 15–20 minutes, or until the meatballs are just cooked. Add the sugar, remaining parsley and oregano and season with salt and freshly cracked pepper.
4 Cook the penne in a large pan of rapidly boiling salted water until *al dente*, then drain. Serve with the hot meatballs.

NUTRITION PER SERVE
Protein 15 g; Fat 8 g; Carbohydrate 60 g; Dietary Fibre 9 g; Cholesterol 60 mg; 1321 kJ (316 cal)

When the veal mixture is thoroughly combined, shape into balls.

Use a very sharp knife to score a shallow cross in the base of each tomato.

Remove the tomatoes from the hot water, plunge into iced water, then peel.

PEPPERED LAMB AND ASPARAGUS STIR-FRY

Fat per serve: 12 g
Preparation time: 35 minutes
  + 20 minutes marinating
Total cooking time: 20 minutes
Serves 4

400 g (13 oz) lamb fillets
2 teaspoons green peppercorns, finely chopped
3 cloves garlic, finely chopped
1 tablespoon vegetable oil
1 onion, cut into small wedges
1/3 cup (80 ml/2³/4 fl oz) dry sherry

1 green capsicum, cut into strips
1/2 teaspoon sugar
16 small asparagus spears, cut into bite-sized pieces, tough ends discarded
200 g (6¹/2 oz) broccoli florets
2 tablespoons oyster sauce
garlic chives, cut into short lengths, to garnish

1 Trim away any sinew from the lamb and cut the lamb into bite-sized pieces. Combine in a bowl with the green peppercorns, garlic and oil, then toss well and set aside for 20 minutes.

2 Heat a wok over high heat until slightly smoking. Add the pieces of lamb and stir-fry in batches until brown and just cooked. Remove, cover and keep warm.

3 Reheat the wok and stir-fry the onion and 2 teaspoons of the sherry for 1 minute. Add the capsicum, sugar and a large pinch of salt. Cover, steam for 2 minutes, add the asparagus, broccoli, then remaining sherry, and stir-fry for 1 minute. Cover and steam for 3 minutes, or until the vegetables are just tender. Return the lamb to the pan, add the oyster sauce and stir to combine with the vegetables. Serve garnished with the chives.

NUTRITION PER SERVE
Protein 25 g; Fat 12 g; Carbohydrate 8 g;
Dietary Fibre 4 g; Cholesterol 65 mg;
1100 kJ (265 cal)

Trim the lamb of any excess fat or sinew, then cut into bite-sized pieces.

Stir-fry the lamb over high heat until brown and just cooked.

Add the asparagus and broccoli to the capsicum and onion.

CHICKEN

CHICKEN AND VEGETABLE LASAGNE

Fat per serve: 10 g
Preparation time: 45 minutes
Total cooking time: 1 hour 20 minutes
Serves 8

500 g (1 lb) chicken breast
   fillets
cooking oil spray
2 cloves garlic, crushed
1 onion, chopped
2 zucchini, chopped
2 celery sticks, chopped
2 carrots, chopped
300 g (10 oz) pumpkin, diced
2 x 400 g (13 oz) cans
   tomatoes, chopped
2 sprigs fresh thyme
2 bay leaves
1/2 cup (125 ml/4 fl oz) white
   wine
2 tablespoons tomato paste
2 tablespoons chopped fresh
   basil
500 g (1 lb) English spinach
500 g (1 lb) reduced-fat cottage
   cheese
450 g (14 oz) ricotta
1/4 cup (60 ml/2 fl oz) skim milk
1/2 teaspoon ground nutmeg
1/3 cup (35 g/1 1/4 oz) grated
   Parmesan
300 g (10 oz) instant or fresh
   lasagne sheets

1 Preheat the oven to moderate 180°C (350°F/Gas 4). Trim excess fat from the chicken breasts, then finely mince in a food processor. Heat a large, deep, non-stick frying pan, spray lightly with oil and cook the chicken mince in batches until browned. Remove and set aside.

2 Add the garlic and onion to the pan and cook until softened. Return the chicken to the pan and add the zucchini, celery, carrot, pumpkin, tomato, thyme, bay leaves, wine and tomato paste. Simmer, covered, for 20 minutes. Remove the bay leaves and thyme, stir in the fresh basil and set aside.

3 Shred the spinach and set aside. Mix the cottage cheese, ricotta, skim milk, nutmeg and half the Parmesan.

4 Spoon a little of the tomato mixture over the base of a casserole dish and top with a single layer of pasta. Top with half the remaining tomato mixture, then the spinach and spoon over half the cottage cheese mixture. Continue with another layer of pasta, the remaining tomato and another layer of pasta. Spread the remaining cottage cheese mixture on top and sprinkle with Parmesan. Bake for 40–50 minutes, or until golden. The top may puff up slightly but will settle on standing.

NUTRITION PER SERVE
Protein 40 g; Fat 10 g; Carbohydrate 35 g; Dietary Fibre 7 g; Cholesterol 70 mg; 1790 kJ (430 cal)

Finely mince the trimmed chicken fillets in a food processor.

Add the vegetables with the bay leaves, thyme, wine and tomato paste to the pan.

WARM CHICKEN SALAD

Fat per serve: 10 g
Preparation time: 30 minutes
  + overnight marinating
Total cooking time: 20 minutes
Serves 4

500 g (1 lb) chicken thigh
    fillets, fat removed
2 teaspoons Thai red curry paste
1 teaspoon chopped red chilli
1 clove garlic, crushed
1 stem fresh lemon grass (white
    part only), finely chopped
cooking oil spray
1 red onion, thinly sliced
2 tomatoes, cut in wedges
1/2 cup (25 g/3/4 oz) chopped
    fresh mint
1/4 cup (15 g/1/2 oz) chopped
    fresh coriander
400 g (13 oz) mixed salad leaves
2 tablespoons roasted peanuts

Dressing
1 1/2 tablespoons soft brown sugar
2 tablespoons fish sauce
2 tablespoons lime juice
2 kaffir lime leaves, shredded
2 teaspoons oil

1 Cut the chicken into thin strips and mix with the curry paste, chilli, garlic and lemon grass. Cover and refrigerate for several hours or overnight.
2 Lightly spray a non-stick frying pan with oil and cook the chicken in batches until tender and lightly browned; set aside. Add the onion to the pan and cook for 1 minute, or until just soft. Return the chicken and any juices to the pan and add the tomato, mint and coriander, stirring until heated. Set aside until just warm.

3 To make the dressing, thoroughly mix the ingredients in a jug. In a large bowl, toss the chicken mixture with the salad leaves and dressing and serve. Sprinkle with the peanuts.

NUTRITION PER SERVE
Protein 25 g; Fat 10 g; Carbohydrate 15 g; Dietary Fibre 2.5 g; Cholesterol 50 mg; 1050 kJ (250 cal)

Remove the fat from the chicken fillets and cut the meat into strips.

If you find it easier, you can use your hands to mix the chicken and marinade.

Stir the tomatoes and herbs with the chicken, until heated through.

CHARGRILLED CHICKEN

Fat per serve: 2.5 g
Preparation time: 20 minutes
+ 2 hours refrigeration
Total cooking time: 1 hour
Serves 4

4 chicken breast fillets
2 tablespoons honey
1 tablespoon wholegrain
    mustard
1 tablespoon soy sauce
2 red onions, cut into wedges

8 Roma tomatoes, halved
    lengthways
2 tablespoons soft brown sugar
2 tablespoons balsamic vinegar
cooking oil spray
snow pea sprouts, for serving

1 Preheat the oven to moderate 180°C (350°F/Gas 4). Trim the chicken of any excess fat and place in a shallow dish. Combine the honey, mustard and soy sauce and pour over the chicken, tossing to coat. Cover and refrigerate for 2 hours, turning once.
2 Place the onion wedges and tomato halves on a baking tray covered with baking paper. Sprinkle with the sugar and drizzle with the balsamic vinegar. Bake for 40 minutes.
3 Heat a chargrill pan and lightly spray with oil. Remove the chicken from the marinade and cook for 4–5 minutes on each side, or until cooked through. Slice and serve with the snow pea sprouts, tomato halves and onion wedges.

NUTRITION PER SERVE
Protein 25 g; Fat 2.5 g; Carbohydrate 30 g; Dietary Fibre 3 g; Cholesterol 50 mg; 990 kJ (235 cal)

Pour the marinade over the chicken and toss to coat thoroughly.

Drizzle the balsamic vinegar over the onion and tomato.

Cook the marinated chicken in a hot, lightly oiled chargrill pan.

CHICKEN PIES

Fat per serve: 10 g
Preparation time: 50 minutes
+ 30 minutes refrigeration
Total cooking time: 1 hour
Serves 4

300 g (10 oz) chicken breast
   fillet
1 bay leaf
2 cups (500 ml/16 oz) chicken
   stock
2 large potatoes, chopped
250 g (8 oz) orange sweet
   potato, chopped
2 celery sticks, chopped
2 carrots, chopped
1 onion, chopped
1 parsnip, chopped
1 clove garlic, crushed
1 tablespoon cornflour
1 cup (250 ml/8 fl oz) skim milk
1 cup (155 g/5 oz) frozen green
   peas, thawed
1 tablespoon chopped fresh
   chives
1 tablespoon chopped fresh
   parsley
1 1/2 cups (185 g/6 oz) self-
   raising flour
20 g (3/4 oz) butter
1/3 cup (80 ml/2 3/4 fl oz) milk
1 egg, lightly beaten
1/2 teaspoon sesame seeds

1 Combine the chicken, bay leaf and stock in a large, deep non-stick frying pan and simmer over low heat for about 10 minutes, until the chicken is cooked through. Remove the chicken, set aside and, when cool, cut into small pieces. Add the chopped potato, orange sweet potato, celery and carrot to the pan and simmer, covered, for about 10 minutes, until just tender. Remove the vegetables from the pan with a slotted spoon.

2 Add the onion, parsnip and garlic to the pan and simmer, uncovered, for about 10 minutes, until very soft. Discard the bay leaf. Purée in a food processor until smooth.

3 Stir the cornflour into 2 tablespoons of the skim milk until it forms a smooth paste, stir into the puréed mixture with the remaining milk and then return to the pan. Stir over low heat until the mixture boils and thickens. Preheat the oven to moderately hot 200°C (400°F/Gas 6).

4 Combine the puréed mixture with the remaining vegetables, chicken and herbs. Season with salt and pepper. Spoon into four 1 3/4 cup (440 ml/ 14 fl oz) capacity ovenproof dishes.

5 To make the pastry, sift the flour into a large bowl, rub in the butter with your fingertips, then make a well in the centre. Combine the milk with 1/3 cup (80 ml/2 3/4 fl oz) water and add enough to the dry ingredients to make a soft dough. Turn out onto a lightly floured surface and knead until just smooth. Cut the dough into four portions and roll each out so that it is 1 cm (1/2 inch) larger than the top of the dish. Brush the edge of the dough with some of the egg and fit over the top of each dish, pressing the edge firmly to seal.

6 Brush the pastry tops lightly with beaten egg and sprinkle with the sesame seeds. Bake for about 30 minutes, until the tops are golden and the filling is heated through.

NUTRITION PER SERVE
Protein 30 g; Fat 10 g; Carbohydrate 65 g; Dietary Fibre 9.5 g; Cholesterol 100 mg; 2045 kJ (490 cal)

Cut the vegetables into even-sized pieces so that they cook at the same rate.

Simmer the chicken in the stock until cooked through.

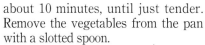

Purée the cooked onion, parsnip and garlic together until smooth.

Stir the sauce constantly until the mixture boils and thickens.

Add enough liquid to the dry ingredients to make a soft dough.

Brush the edge of the dough with egg, then press over the top of each dish.

CHICKEN MOLE

Fat per serve: 7 g
Preparation time: about 25 minutes
Total cooking time: 1 hour
Serves 4

8 chicken drumsticks (1.6 kg)
plain flour, for dusting
cooking oil spray
1 large onion, finely chopped
2 cloves garlic, finely chopped
1 teaspoon ground cumin
1 teaspoon Mexican chilli powder
2 teaspoons cocoa powder
440 g (14 oz) can tomatoes,
    roughly chopped

440 ml (14 fl oz) tomato purée
1 cup (250 ml/8 fl oz) chicken
    stock
toasted almonds and chopped
    parsley, to garnish

1 Remove and discard the chicken skin. Wipe the chicken with paper towels and lightly dust with flour. Spray a large, deep, non-stick pan with oil. Cook the chicken for 8 minutes over high heat, turning until golden brown. Remove and set aside.

2 Add the onion, garlic, cumin, chilli powder, cocoa, 1 teaspoon salt, 1/2 teaspoon black pepper and 1/4 cup (60 ml/2 fl oz) water to the pan and cook for 5 minutes, or until softened.

3 Stir in the tomato, tomato purée and chicken stock. Bring to the boil, add the chicken drumsticks, cover and simmer for 45 minutes, or until tender. Uncover and simmer for 5 minutes, until the mixture is thick. Garnish with the almonds and parsley. Shown here with kidney beans.

NUTRITION PER SERVE
Protein 25 g; Fat 7 g; Carbohydrate 10 g; Dietary Fibre 4 g; Cholesterol 100 mg; 910 kJ (220 cal)

COOK'S FILE

Note: This is a traditional Mexican dish, usually flavoured with a special type of dark chocolate rather than cocoa powder.

Pull the skin off the chicken drumsticks, then wipe the chicken with paper towels.

Turn the chicken until brown on all sides, then remove from the pan.

Stir in the onion, garlic, cumin, chilli powder, cocoa, salt, pepper and water.

LEMON GRASS CHICKEN SKEWERS

Fat per serve: 2.5 g
Preparation time: 20 minutes
  + overnight marinating
Total cooking time: 15–20 minutes
Serves 4

4 chicken thigh fillets
   (400 g/13 oz)
1¹/2 tablespoons soft brown sugar
1¹/2 tablespoons lime juice
2 teaspoons green curry paste
18 kaffir lime leaves
2 stems lemon grass

Mango salsa
1 small mango, finely diced
1 teaspoon grated lime rind
2 teaspoons lime juice
1 teaspoon soft brown sugar
¹/2 teaspoon fish sauce

1 Discard any excess fat from the chicken fillets and cut them in half lengthways. Combine the brown sugar, lime juice, curry paste and 2 of the kaffir lime leaves, shredded, in a bowl. Add the chicken and mix well. Cover and refrigerate for several hours or overnight.
2 Trim the lemon grass to measure about 20 cm (8 inches), leaving the root end intact. Cut each lengthways into four pieces. Cut a slit in each of the remaining lime leaves and thread one onto each skewer. Cut two slits in the chicken and thread onto the lemon grass, followed by another lime leaf. Repeat with the remaining lime leaves, chicken and lemon grass. Pan-fry or barbecue until cooked through.
3 To make the mango salsa, put all the ingredients in a bowl and stir gently to combine. Serve with the chicken skewers.

NUTRITION PER SERVE
Protein 25 g; Fat 2.5 g; Carbohydrate 15 g; Dietary Fibre 1 g; Cholesterol 50 mg; 710 kJ (170 cal)

Discard any excess fat from the chicken thighs and cut in half lengthways.

Cut each trimmed lemon grass stem lengthways into four pieces.

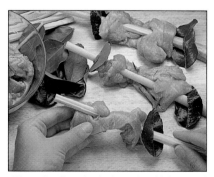

Thread a lime leaf, then the chicken and another lime leaf onto the lemon grass.

CHICKEN CACCIATORE

Fat per serve: 6 g
Preparation time: 25 minutes
Total cooking time: 40 minutes
Serves 4

500 g (1 lb) chicken breast fillets
plain flour, for dusting
2 teaspoons olive oil
2 onions, finely sliced
2 cloves garlic, finely chopped
2 anchovy fillets, chopped
440 g (14 oz) can chopped
    tomatoes

125 ml (4 fl oz) dry white wine
3 tablespoons tomato paste
1 teaspoon soft brown sugar
6 Kalamata olives, pitted and
    chopped
chopped fresh parsley, to garnish

1 Trim the fat from the chicken and lightly dust the chicken in plain flour. Heat the oil in a large, heavy-based non-stick frying pan and cook the chicken over high heat for 10 minutes, turning until golden and almost cooked. (If the chicken begins to stick, sprinkle with water and reduce the heat.) Remove, cover and set aside.

2 Add the onion to the pan with the garlic, anchovies and 1 tablespoon of water. Cover and cook for 5 minutes, stirring. Add the tomato, wine, tomato paste, sugar and 200 ml (7 fl oz) water. Bring to the boil, reduce the heat and simmer for 20 minutes. Season.

3 Return the chicken and juices to the pan. Add the olives and simmer for 5 minutes, or until the chicken is heated through. Garnish with parsley. Delicious with fusilli or other pasta.

NUTRITION PER SERVE
Protein 30 g; Fat 6 g; Carbohydrate 10 g;
Dietary Fibre 3 g; Cholesterol 60 mg;
985 kJ (235 cal)

Trim any fat from the chicken and dust the fillets lightly with flour.

Sprinkling with a little water will help prevent the chicken sticking.

When the tomato sauce is cooked, return the chicken and juices to the pan.

CHICKEN WITH BAKED EGGPLANT AND TOMATO

Fat per serve: 4.5 g
Preparation time: 30 minutes
Total cooking time: 1 hour 30 minutes
Serves 4

1 red capsicum
1 eggplant
3 tomatoes, cut into quarters
200 g (6½ oz) large button
   mushrooms, halved
1 onion, cut into thin wedges
1½ tablespoons tomato paste
½ cup (125 ml/4 fl oz) chicken
   stock

¼ cup (60 ml/2 fl oz) white wine
2 lean bacon rashers
4 chicken breast fillets
   (500 g/1 lb)
4 small sprigs fresh rosemary
cooking oil spray

1 Preheat the oven to moderately hot 200°C (400°F/Gas 6). Cut the capsicum and eggplant into bite-sized pieces and combine with the tomato, mushrooms and onion in a baking dish. Spray with oil and bake for 1 hour, or until starting to brown and soften, stirring once.
2 Pour the combined tomato paste, stock and wine into the dish and bake for 10 minutes, or until thickened.

3 Meanwhile, discard the fat and rind from the bacon and cut in half. Wrap a strip around each chicken breast and secure it underneath with a toothpick. Poke a sprig of fresh rosemary underneath the bacon. Pan-fry in a lightly oiled, non-stick frying pan, over medium heat, until golden on both sides. Cover and cook for 10–15 minutes, or until the chicken is tender and cooked through. Remove the toothpicks. Serve the chicken on the vegetable mixture, surrounded with sauce.

NUTRITION PER SERVE
Protein 35 g; Fat 4.5 g; Carbohydrate 8 g; Dietary Fibre 5 g; Cholesterol 70 mg; 965 kJ (230 cal)

Spray the vegetables lightly with cooking oil before baking.

When the vegetables have softened, add the tomato paste, wine and stock.

Wrap a strip of bacon around the chicken and secure underneath with a toothpick.

SEAFOOD

FISH BURGERS WITH TARTARE SAUCE

Fat per serve: 15 g
Preparation time: 30 minutes
  + 1 hour refrigeration
Total cooking time: 25 minutes
Serves 4

500 g (1 lb) white fish fillets
2 tablespoons finely chopped
    fresh parsley
2 tablespoons finely chopped
    fresh dill
2 tablespoons lemon juice
1 tablespoon capers, finely
    chopped
2 finely chopped gherkins
350 g (12 oz) potatoes, cooked
    and mashed
plain flour, for dusting
2 teaspoons olive oil
4 hamburger buns
lettuce leaves
2 Roma tomatoes, sliced

Tartare sauce
1/3 cup (90 g/3 oz) low-fat
    mayonnaise
1/2 finely chopped gherkin
2 teaspoons capers, finely
    chopped
1/2 teaspoon malt vinegar
2 teaspoons finely chopped
    fresh parsley
2 teaspoons lemon juice

1 Place the fish fillets in a frying pan and just cover with water. Slowly heat the water, making sure it doesn't boil. Cover and cook over low heat until the fish is just cooked. Drain the fish on paper towels, transfer to a large bowl and flake with a fork. Add the parsley, dill, lemon juice, capers, gherkin and mashed potato, season well with freshly cracked pepper and salt and mix until well combined. Divide into four portions and shape into patties, handling the mixture carefully as it is quite soft. Dust lightly with flour and refrigerate on a plate for 1 hour.

2 Meanwhile, make the tartare sauce by mixing all the ingredients thoroughly in a bowl.

3 Heat the olive oil in a large non-stick frying pan, carefully add the patties and cook for 5–6 minutes on each side, or until well browned and heated through.

4 Meanwhile, cut the hamburger buns in half and toast under a grill. On each bun base, put some lettuce leaves, a few slices of tomato, a patty and finally, a quarter of the tartare sauce. Cover with the bun tops and serve. The recipe for the crunchy potato wedges shown in the picture is on page 64.

NUTRITION PER SERVE
Protein 40 g; Fat 15 g; Carbohydrate 70 g; Dietary Fibre 7 g; Cholesterol 95 mg; 2375 kJ (565 cal)

Pour in enough water to cover the fish fillets and slowly heat the water.

Mix the flaked fish with the herbs, potato, juice, capers, gherkin and seasoning.

SARDINES WITH CHARGRILLED CAPSICUM AND EGGPLANT

Fat per serve: 15 g
Preparation time: 25 minutes
Total cooking time: 35 minutes
Serves 4

2 large red capsicums,
    quartered and seeded
4 finger eggplants, cut into
    quarters lengthways
cooking oil spray

Dressing
1 tablespoon olive oil
1 tablespoon balsamic vinegar
1/2 teaspoon soft brown sugar
1 clove garlic, crushed
1 tablespoon chopped fresh
    chives

16 fresh sardines, butterflied
    (about 300 g/10 oz)
1 slice white bread, crusts
    removed
1/3 cup (7 g/1/4 oz) fresh parsley
1 clove garlic, crushed
1 teaspoon grated lemon rind

1 Preheat the oven to moderate 180°C (350°F/Gas 4). Lightly grease a large baking dish with oil. Preheat the grill and line with foil.
2 Grill the capsicum until the skin is blistered and blackened. Cool under a damp tea towel, peel and slice thickly lengthways. Lightly spray the eggplant with oil and grill each side for 3–5 minutes, until softened.
3 Combine the dressing ingredients in a jar and shake well. Put the capsicum and eggplant in a bowl, pour the dressing over, toss well and set aside.

4 Place the sardines on a baking tray in a single layer, well spaced. Finely chop the bread, parsley, garlic and lemon rind together in a food processor. Sprinkle over each sardine. Bake for 10–15 minutes, until cooked through. Serve the capsicum and eggplant topped with sardines.

NUTRITION PER SERVE
Protein 20 g; Fat 15 g; Carbohydrate 15 g;
Dietary Fibre 3 g; Cholesterol 85 mg;
1185 kJ (285 cal)

When the capsicum has cooled enough to handle, peel away the skin.

Pour the dressing over the capsicum and eggplant, then toss.

Sprinkle the chopped bread, parsley, garlic and lemon rind over the sardines.

TUNA KEBABS

Fat per serve: 15 g
Preparation time: 20 minutes
Total cooking time: 20 minutes
Serves 4

1 tablespoon olive oil
2–3 small red chillies, seeded
   and finely chopped
3–4 cloves garlic, crushed
1 red onion, finely chopped
3 tomatoes, seeded and chopped
1/4 cup (60 ml/2 fl oz) white
   wine or water

2 x 300 g (10 oz) cans chickpeas
1/4 cup (7 g/1/4 oz) chopped fresh
   oregano
1/3 cup (20 g/3/4 oz) chopped
   fresh parsley

Tuna kebabs
1 kg (2 lb) tuna fillet, cut into
   4 cm (11/2 inch) cubes
8 stalks of rosemary, about 20 cm
   (8 inch) long, with leaves
cooking oil spray
lemon wedges, to serve

1 Heat the oil in a large pan, add the
chilli, garlic and red onion and stir for

5 minutes, or until softened. Add the
tomato and wine or water. Cook over
low heat for 10 minutes, or until the
mixture is soft, pulpy and the liquid
has evaporated. Stir in the rinsed
chickpeas, oregano and parsley. Season.
2 Heat a grill or barbecue plate.
Thread the tuna onto the rosemary
stalks, lightly spray with oil, then
cook, turning, for 3 minutes. Do not
overcook or the tuna will fall apart.
Serve with the chickpeas and lemon.

NUTRITION PER SERVE
Protein 75 g; Fat 15 g; Carbohydrate 25 g;
Dietary Fibre 10 g; Cholesterol 110 mg;
2355 kJ (565 cal)

*Stir the chopped chilli, red onion and the
crushed garlic until softened.*

*Drain the chickpeas and rinse well before
adding to the pan.*

*Thread the tuna pieces onto the long
rosemary stalks.*

CRUMBED FISH WITH WASABI CREAM

Fat per serve: 6 g
Preparation time: 25 minutes
  + 15 minutes refrigeration
Total cooking time: 20 minutes
Serves 4

3/4 cup (60 g/2 oz) fresh
    breadcrumbs
3/4 cup (25 g/3/4 oz) cornflakes
1 sheet nori, torn roughly
1/4 teaspoon paprika
4 x 150 g (5 oz) pieces firm
    white fish fillets
plain flour, for dusting
1 egg white
1 tablespoon skim milk
1 spring onion, thinly sliced

Wasabi cream
1/2 cup (125 ml/4 oz) low-fat
    natural yoghurt
1 teaspoon wasabi (see note)
1 tablespoon light mayonnaise
1 teaspoon lime juice

1 Preheat the oven to moderate 180°C
(350°F/Gas 4). Combine the crumbs,
cornflakes, nori and paprika in a food
processor and process until the nori is
finely chopped.
2 Dust the fish lightly with plain
flour, dip into the combined egg white
and milk, then into the breadcrumb
mixture. Press the crumb mixture on
firmly, then refrigerate for 15 minutes.
3 Line a baking tray with non-stick
baking paper and put the fish on the
paper. Bake for 15–20 minutes, or
until the fish flakes easily when tested
with a fork.
4 To make the wasabi cream, mix the
ingredients thoroughly in a bowl.

Serve a spoonful on top of the fish
and sprinkle with spring onion.

NUTRITION PER SERVE
Protein 35 g; Fat 6 g; Carbohydrate 25 g;
Dietary Fibre 1 g; Cholesterol 105 mg;
1270 kJ (305 cal)

COOK'S FILE

Note: Wasabi paste (a pungent paste,
also known as Japanese horseradish)
and nori (sheets of paper-thin dried
seaweed) are both available from
Japanese food stores.

*Process the breadcrumbs, cornflakes, nori
and paprika together.*

*Dust the fish with flour, dip in the egg
and milk, then press in the breadcrumbs.*

*Thoroughly mix the wasabi cream
ingredients in a bowl.*

STEAMED TROUT WITH GINGER AND CORIANDER

Fat per serve: 10 g
Preparation time: 20 minutes
Total cooking time: 30 minutes
Serves 2

2 whole rainbow trout (about
   330 g/11 oz each), cleaned
   and scaled
2 limes, thinly sliced
5 cm (2 inch) piece ginger, cut
   into matchsticks
1/4 cup (60 g/2 oz) caster sugar
1/4 cup (60 ml/2 fl oz) lime juice
rind of 1 lime, cut in thin strips
1/3 cup (10 g/1/4 oz) fresh
   coriander leaves

1 Preheat the oven to moderate 180°C (350°F/Gas 4). Fill the fish cavities with the lime slices and some of the ginger, then place the fish on a large piece of lightly greased foil. Wrap the fish and bake on a baking tray for 20–30 minutes, until the flesh flakes easily when tested with a fork.
2 Combine the sugar and lime juice with 250 ml (8 fl oz) water in a small pan and stir without boiling until the sugar dissolves. Bring to the boil, reduce the heat and simmer for 10 minutes, or until syrupy. Stir in the remaining ginger and lime strips. Put the fish on a plate. Top with coriander leaves and pour the hot syrup over it.

NUTRITION PER SERVE
Protein 50 g; Fat 10 g; Carbohydrate 30 g; Dietary Fibre 1 g; Cholesterol 120 mg; 1715 kJ (410 cal)

COOK'S FILE

Note: You can ask the fishmonger to remove the bones from the fish.

Peel the ginger and cut it into fine, short matchsticks.

Fill the cavities of the trout with the lime slices and some of the ginger.

Simmer the sugar in the lime juice and water until syrupy.

NOODLE SALAD

Fat per serve: 8 g
Preparation time: 35 minutes
Total cooking time: 10 minutes
Serves 4–6

500g (1 lb) fresh udon noodles
2 teaspoons sesame oil
3 cloves garlic, finely chopped
4 cm (1¹/2 inch) piece ginger,
    finely chopped
200 g (6¹/2 oz) broccoli, cut into
    small pieces
2 carrots, cut into matchsticks
100 g (3 oz) snow peas, sliced
    into long, thin strips
1 cup (90 g/3 oz) bean sprouts
¹/4 cup (15 g/¹/2 oz) chopped
    fresh coriander
2 tablespoons Japanese mirin
3 tablespoons low-salt soy sauce
8 cooked king prawns, peeled
    and deveined, tails intact
2 teaspoons sesame seeds,
    toasted
sliced spring onions, to garnish

1 Cook the udon noodles in a large pan of boiling water for 5 minutes, or until tender. Drain and rinse in cold water until cold to prevent them sticking together. Transfer to a large bowl and cut into small pieces, using scissors. Toss 1 teaspoon of the sesame oil through, cover and set aside.
2 Heat the remaining sesame oil in a small pan, add the garlic and ginger and cook over low heat for 5 minutes, stirring occasionally. Remove from the heat, cool and add to the noodles.
3 Bring a large pan of water to the boil and add the prepared broccoli, carrot and snow peas. Return to the boil, reduce the heat and simmer for

1 minute. Drain in a colander and rinse under cold water until the vegetables are cold. Drain.
4 Add the blanched vegetables, bean sprouts, coriander, mirin, soy sauce and prawns to the noodles. Toss until well combined. Transfer to a serving bowl and sprinkle with sesame seeds and spring onion. Serve immediately.

NUTRITION PER SERVE (6)
Protein 20 g; Fat 8 g; Carbohydrate 65 g; Dietary Fibre 8 g; Cholesterol 35 mg; 1690 kJ (405 cal)

COOK'S FILE

Note: Udon noodles and mirin are available from Japanese or Asian food stores and some supermarkets.

Use scissors to cut the udon noodles into pieces so they are easier to eat.

Cook the chopped garlic and ginger in the sesame oil for about 5 minutes.

Blanch the prepared broccoli, carrot and snow peas.

FUSILLI WITH TUNA, CAPERS AND PARSLEY

Fat per serve: 13 g
Preparation time: 15 minutes
Total cooking time: 10 minutes
Serves 4

425 g (14 oz) can tuna in spring
   water, drained
2 tablespoons olive oil
2 cloves garlic, finely chopped
2 small red chillies, finely
   chopped

3 tablespoons capers
1/2 cup (30 g/1 oz) finely
   chopped fresh parsley
3 tablespoons lemon juice
375 g (12 oz) fusilli

1 Place the drained tuna in a bowl and flake lightly with a fork. In a small bowl, combine the oil, garlic, chilli, capers, parsley and lemon juice. Pour over the tuna and mix lightly. Season well with salt and freshly ground black pepper.

2 Meanwhile, cook the pasta in a large pan of rapidly boiling salted water for 10 minutes, or until *al dente*. Reserve 1/2 cup (125 ml/4 fl oz) of the cooking water, then drain the pasta. Toss the tuna mixture through the pasta, adding enough of the reserved water to give a moist consistency. Serve immediately.

NUTRITION PER SERVE
Protein 35 g; Fat 13 g; Carbohydrate 65 g;
Dietary Fibre 5 g; Cholesterol 55 mg;
2270 kJ (545 cal)

COOK'S FILE

Hint: Generally, the smaller the caper the tastier, so use baby ones if possible.

Finely chop the chillies. Remove the seeds if you prefer a milder taste.

Break the well-drained tuna into flakes with a fork.

Add the pasta gradually to a large pan of rapidly boiling salted water.

SEAFOOD AND HERB RISOTTO

Fat per serve: 5 g
Preparation time: 40 minutes
Total cooking time: 45–50 minutes
Serves 4

150 g (5 oz) white boneless fish
  fillet such as sea perch
8 black mussels (200 g/6½ oz)
8 raw prawns (250 g/8 oz)
1.75 litres chicken stock
cooking oil spray
2 onions, finely chopped
2 cloves garlic, finely chopped
1 celery stick, finely chopped
2 cups (440 g/14 oz) arborio
  rice
2 tablespoons chopped fresh
  parsley
1 tablespoon chopped fresh
  oregano
1 tablespoon chopped fresh
  thyme leaves
2 tablespoons freshly grated
  Parmesan

1 Cut the fish fillet into small cubes. Scrub the mussels well and remove the beards. Discard any mussels that are not tightly closed. Peel and devein the prawns, leaving the tails intact. Put the seafood in a bowl and refrigerate until required.

2 Put the stock in a saucepan and bring to the boil, then reduce the heat until just gently simmering.

3 Lightly spray a large saucepan with cooking oil and heat over medium heat. Add the onion, garlic and celery and cook for 2–3 minutes. Add 2 tablespoons water, cover and cook for 5 minutes, or until the vegetables have begun to soften. Add the arborio rice as well as 2 tablespoons water, cover and continue to cook over medium heat for 3–4 minutes, or until the rice grains are well coated.

4 Gradually add ½ cup (125 ml/4 fl oz) of the hot stock to the rice mixture, stirring constantly over low heat with a wooden spoon, until all the stock has been absorbed. Repeat the process, adding ½ cup of liquid each time until all but a small amount of stock is left and the rice is just tender.

5 Meanwhile, bring a small amount of water to the boil in a saucepan. Add the mussels, cover and cook for about 3 minutes, shaking the pan occasionally, until the mussels have opened. Drain the mussels and discard any that have not opened. Set aside.

6 Add the fish and prawns and the remaining hot stock to the rice. Stir well and continue to cook for about 5–10 minutes, or until the seafood is just cooked and the rice is tender and creamy. Remove from the heat, add the cooked mussels, cover and set aside for 5 minutes. Stir the herbs and Parmesan through the risotto, then season well with freshly cracked pepper and salt. Serve immediately in individual bowls.

NUTRITION PER SERVE
Protein 40 g; Fat 5 g; Carbohydrate 90 g; Dietary Fibre 4 g; Cholesterol 175 mg; 2395 kJ (570 cal)

COOK'S FILE

Note: Arborio rice has a fatter and shorter grain than regular short-grain rice. The chief ingredient of risotto, arborio has a high starch content which gives the dish its creamy texture. This is the reason it can't be successfully substituted with any other type of rice.

Scrub the mussels thoroughly and pull off the beards.

Add the arborio rice to the pan, cover and cook until the rice is well coated.

Stir a little of the hot stock at a time into the rice until it is all absorbed.

Risotto is ready when the rice has absorbed all the hot stock.

Put the mussels in a pan of boiling water, cover and cook until they open.

Stir the chopped herbs and grated Parmesan through the risotto.

CALAMARI WITH SPICY SAUCE

Fat per serve: 6.5 g
Preparation time: 50 minutes
  + 3 hours marinating
Total cooking time: 7 minutes
Serves 4

500 g (1 lb) calamari tubes,
    cleaned
2 stems lemon grass, white part
    only, finely chopped
3 teaspoons grated ginger
3 cloves garlic, finely chopped
1/2 teaspoon chopped fresh red
    chilli
1 tablespoon vegetable oil
2 very ripe tomatoes
150 g (5 oz) mixed lettuce
1/4 cup (7 g/1/4 oz) fresh
    coriander leaves
2 tablespoons lime juice
1 teaspoon finely grated lime rind
1 red capsicum, cut into strips

Lime, chilli and garlic sauce
1/4 cup (60 ml/2 fl oz) lime juice
1 tablespoon lemon juice
2 tablespoons fish sauce
1 tablespoon caster sugar
2 teaspoons chopped fresh
    red chilli
2 cloves garlic, finely chopped
1 tablespoon finely chopped
    fresh coriander

1 Cut the calamari tubes open, wash and pat dry. Cut shallow slashes about 5 mm (1/4 inch) apart on the soft inside, in a diamond pattern, then cut into 3 cm (1 1/4 inch) strips. Mix in a bowl with the lemon grass, ginger, garlic, chilli and oil. Cover with plastic wrap and refrigerate for 3 hours.

2 Cut the tomatoes in half, scoop out the membrane and seeds and finely chop them, retaining all the juices. Cut the flesh into small cubes and set aside. Arrange the lettuce and coriander leaves in serving bowls.

3 Just before serving, lightly grease and heat a solid barbecue plate or large, heavy non-stick pan until very hot. Quickly cook the calamari in batches, tossing for 2–3 minutes, until just tender and curled, sprinkling the lime juice and rind over the top. Remove the calamari, toss with the chopped tomato seeds and arrange on the salad. Scatter the tomato and capsicum over the top. Season well.

4 Stir the sauce ingredients together until the sugar dissolves. Drizzle over the calamari.

NUTRITION PER SERVE
Protein 25 g; Fat 6.5 g; Carbohydrate 5 g; Dietary Fibre 3 g; Cholesterol 250 mg; 755 kJ (180 cal)

Score a shallow diamond pattern on the soft insides of the calamari tubes.

Scoop out the tomato membrane and seeds and finely chop them.

Don't overcook the calamari or it will be tough, and don't crowd the pan.

JAPANESE-STYLE SALMON PARCELS

Fat per serve: 14 g
Preparation time: 40 minutes
Total cooking time: 15 minutes
Serves 4

2 teaspoons sesame seeds
4 x 150 g (5 oz) salmon
 cutlets or steaks
2.5 cm (1 inch) piece ginger
2 celery sticks
4 spring onions
1/4 teaspoon dashi granules
3 tablespoons mirin
2 tablespoons tamari

1 Cut baking paper into four squares large enough to enclose the salmon steaks. Preheat the oven to very hot 230°C (450°F/Gas 8). Lightly toast the sesame seeds.
2 Wash the salmon and dry with paper towels. Place a salmon cutlet in the centre of each paper square.
3 Cut the ginger into paper-thin slices. Slice the celery and spring onions into short lengths, then lengthways into fine strips. Arrange a bundle of the prepared strips and several slices of ginger on each salmon steak.
4 Combine the dashi granules, mirin and tamari in a small saucepan. Heat gently until the granules dissolve.

Drizzle over each parcel, sprinkle with sesame seeds and carefully wrap the salmon, folding in the sides to seal in all the juices. Arrange the parcels on a baking tray and cook for about 12 minutes, or until tender. (The paper will puff up when the fish is cooked.) Do not overcook or the salmon will dry out. Serve immediately, as standing time can spoil the fish.

NUTRITION PER SERVE
Protein 20 g; Fat 14 g; Carbohydrate 0 g; Dietary Fibre 0.5 g; Cholesterol 85 mg; 935 kJ (225 cal)

COOK'S FILE

Note: Dashi, mirin and tamari are all available from Japanese food stores.

Cut the celery sticks into short lengths, then lengthways into thin strips.

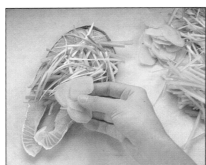

Arrange celery and spring onion strips on the fish and top with ginger slices.

Wrap the salmon in baking paper, folding the sides to seal in the juices.

From top left: Sweet potato crisps; Baked hash browns; Mushrooms with leek and cheese.

Vegetables

By using a minimal amount of oil, vegetables can be cooked your favourite way, taste good and still have a low fat content. And hold the mayonnaise—try low-fat yoghurt instead.

SWEET POTATO CRISPS

Peel an orange sweet potato and cut it into very thin slices. Put the slices in a large bowl of iced water with 1 teaspoon of salt. Set aside for 30 minutes, then drain, spread in a single layer on a lightly greased baking tray and spray lightly with cooking oil. Bake at moderately hot 200°C (400°F/Gas 6) for 30 minutes, turning after 15 minutes. Remove from the tray as soon as they are brown and crisp. Sprinkle while hot with 1 teaspoon dried parsley flakes combined with 1 teaspoon salt, 1/2 teaspoon paprika, a pinch of caster

sugar and 1/4 teaspoon ground cumin. Toss well and store in an airtight container for 3–4 days. Serves 4.

NUTRITION PER SERVE
Protein 1 g; Fat 0 g; Carbohydrate 10 g; Dietary Fibre 1 g; Cholesterol 0 mg; 235 kJ (55 cal)

CRUNCHY WEDGES

Preheat the oven to moderately hot 200°C (400°F/Gas 6). Cut 6 potatoes into 8 wedges each. Dry, then toss with 1 tablespoon oil. Combine 1/2 teaspoon chicken or vegetable stock powder, 1/4 cup (25 g/3/4 oz) dry breadcrumbs, 2 teaspoons chopped

fresh chives, 1 teaspoon celery salt, 1/4 teaspoon garlic powder and 1/2 teaspoon chopped fresh rosemary. Add the wedges and toss. Spread on greased baking trays and bake for 40 minutes, or until golden. Serves 6.

NUTRITION PER SERVE
Protein 3.5 g; Fat 0 g; Carbohydrate 20 g; Dietary Fibre 2 g; Cholesterol 0 mg; 515 kJ (125 cal)

BAKED HASH BROWNS

Preheat the oven to moderately hot 200°C (400°F/Gas 6). Cut 3 potatoes (600 g/1 1/4 lb) in half and boil for 10 minutes—the potatoes will be just

From bottom left: Crunchy wedges; Baked vegetables; Grilled potatoes with garlic cream.

tender on the outside and firm in the centre. Remove from the pan, cool, then coarsely grate and divide into six portions. Using wet hands, shape into flat patties. Spray a non-stick baking tray lightly with oil. Arrange the hash browns on the tray, and spray lightly with olive oil. Bake for 20 minutes, turn and cook for 5–10 minutes, until crisp and golden. Serves 6.

NUTRITION PER SERVE
Protein 2.5 g; Fat 1 g; Carbohydrate 13 g; Dietary Fibre 1.5 g; Cholesterol 0 mg; 275 kJ (65 cal)

BAKED VEGETABLES

Preheat the oven to moderately hot 200°C (400°F/Gas 6). Cut 2 carrots and 2 parsnips in half lengthways, then crossways. Quarter 2 large potatoes. Cut 300 g (10 oz) pumpkin into chunks. Put the vegetables in a baking dish and spray lightly with cooking oil. Sprinkle with salt and cracked black pepper and bake for

20 minutes, turning occasionally. Cut 2 finger eggplants in half lengthways and make thin shallow cuts through the skin. Add to the dish and cook, turning occasionally, for 20 minutes, or until the vegetables are tender. Sprinkle with parsley. Serves 4.

NUTRITION PER SERVE
Protein 5.5 g; Fat 1 g; Carbohydrate 25 g; Dietary Fibre 6 g; Cholesterol 0 mg; 535 kJ (130 cal)

MUSHROOMS WITH LEEK AND CHEESE

Preheat the oven to moderately hot 200°C (400°F/Gas 6). Chop the stalks from 6 cap mushrooms. In a pan, cook the mushroom stalks and 1 finely sliced leek (white part only) with 2 teaspoons butter and 2 teaspoons water, stirring until very soft. Season and spoon into the mushroom caps. Sprinkle with a mixture of 1 1/2 tablespoons fresh breadcrumbs, 1 1/2 tablespoons grated Parmesan

and 1 1/2 tablespoons chopped fresh parsley. Bake for 20 minutes, or until golden. Serves 6.

NUTRITION PER MUSHROOM
Protein 2.5 g; Fat 2 g; Carbohydrate 2 g; Dietary Fibre 1.5 g; Cholesterol 6.5 mg; 160 kJ (40 cal)

GRILLED POTATOES WITH GARLIC CREAM

Cook 4 potatoes until tender. Drain. When cold, cut into 1 cm (1/2 inch) slices. Brown both sides on a lightly greased griddle pan or barbecue. Serve hot with 1/4 cup (60 g/2 oz) light sour cream combined with 100 g (3 1/2 oz) low-fat natural yoghurt, 2 cloves crushed garlic, 1/4 teaspoon paprika and 1 tablespoon chopped garlic chives. Sprinkle with parsley and a little chopped red capsicum. Serves 4.

NUTRITION PER SERVE
Protein 5 g; Fat 3 g; Carbohydrate 20 g; Dietary Fibre 2 g; Cholesterol 10 mg; 525 kJ (125 cal)

65

SPRING ROLLS WITH PRAWN AND VEGETABLE

Fat per spring roll: 1 g
Preparation time: 50 minutes
Total cooking time: 4 minutes
Makes about 18 spring rolls

50 g (1³/4 oz) rice vermicelli
2 spring onions
1 Lebanese cucumber, peeled
1 carrot
24 cooked prawns, peeled and
　　chopped
2 tablespoons chopped roasted
　　unsalted peanuts
2 Chinese mushrooms, soaked,
　　chopped finely
1/2 lettuce, finely shredded
1/2 cup (25 g/³/4 oz) chopped
　　fresh mint
50 g (1³/4 oz) bean sprouts
375 g (12 oz) rice paper rounds,
　　21 cm (8¹/2 inch) diameter

Dipping sauce
2 tablespoons caster sugar
2 tablespoons fish sauce
2 tablespoons lime juice
1 tablespoon rice vinegar or
　　white vinegar
1 spring onion, finely chopped
1 small red chilli, seeded and
　　finely chopped
1 clove garlic, crushed

1 Put the vermicelli in a bowl, cover with boiling water and leave for 1–2 minutes, or until soft. Rinse under cold water, drain, chop roughly with scissors and put in a bowl.
2 Very finely shred the spring onions, cucumber and carrot into thin 5 cm (2 inch) strips. Blanch the carrot in boiling water for 1 minute, drain and cool. Add them all to the cooled vermicelli with the prawns, peanuts, mushrooms, lettuce, mint and bean sprouts. Toss, using your hands.
3 For each spring roll, soften a rice paper in a bowl of warm water for 10–20 seconds. Lay it on a tea towel and place 3 tablespoons of filling in the centre. Fold in the sides and roll up into a parcel. Seal the edges by brushing with a little water. Place on a serving platter and cover with a damp cloth. Repeat until all the ingredients are used.
4 To make the dipping sauce, combine the sugar and 2 tablespoons warm water in a small bowl and stir until the sugar dissolves. Add the remaining ingredients and stir well. Serve with the spring roll.

NUTRITION PER SPRING ROLL
Protein 6 g; Fat 1 g; Carbohydrate 5 g; Dietary Fibre 1 g; Cholesterol 35 mg; 246 kJ (60 cal)

The spring onion, cucumber and carrot should be cut into short, fine strips.

Soften one sheet of rice paper at a time in a bowl of warm water.

Put the filling in the centre of the rice paper, then roll and fold into a parcel.

PRAWN FRIED RICE

Fat per serve: 3 g
Preparation time: 20 minutes
Total cooking time: 15 minutes
Serves 6

4 egg whites, lightly beaten
cooking oil spray
2 cloves garlic, crushed
350 g (12 oz) raw prawns,
    peeled, deveined and
    halved lengthways
100 g (3¹/2 oz) cooked chicken,
    shredded

¹/2 cup (80 g/2³/4 oz) frozen peas
180 g (6 oz) sliced light ham,
    cut into small strips
1 red capsicum, diced
4 spring onions, sliced
4 cups (750 g/1¹/2 lb) cooked
    white and wild rice blend
1¹/2 tablespoons soy sauce
3 teaspoons fish sauce
1¹/2 teaspoons soft brown sugar

1 Lightly spray a non-stick wok with oil and pour in the egg white. Cook over low heat, stirring until the egg is just cooked and slightly scrambled, then remove and set aside.

2 Add the garlic, prawns, chicken, peas, ham and capsicum to the wok and stir-fry for 3–4 minutes, or until the prawns are cooked.
3 Add the spring onion, rice, soy and fish sauces and sugar and toss for 30 seconds, or until heated through. Add the egg, toss lightly and serve.

NUTRITION PER SERVE
Protein 35 g; Fat 3 g; Carbohydrate 105 g; Dietary Fibre 4 g; Cholesterol 120 mg; 2500 kJ (600 cal)

COOK'S FILE

Hint: You will need to cook 1¹/3 cups (260 g/8 oz) rice for this recipe.

Stir the egg white over low heat until just cooked and slightly scrambled.

Stir-fry the garlic, prawns, chicken, capsicum, peas and ham.

When the prawns are cooked, add the rice, spring onion, sauces and sugar.

PAELLA

Fat per serve: 3.5 g
Preparation time: 30 minutes
Total cooking time: 40 minutes
Serves 4

3–4 small calamari
12 mussels
1/2 cup (125 ml/4 fl oz) white
    wine
1 onion, finely chopped
2 teaspoons olive oil
1 chicken breast fillet
    (125 g/4 oz), cubed
4 cloves garlic, crushed
1 red capsicum, cut into strips
1 tomato, peeled and chopped
1/2 cup (80 g/2³/4 oz) peas
60 g (2 oz) cabanossi, finely sliced
pinch cayenne pepper
1 cup (200 g/6¹/2 oz) long-grain
    rice
1/4 teaspoon powdered saffron
2 cups (500 ml/16 fl oz) hot
    chicken stock
100 g (3¹/2 oz) boneless white
    fish fillet, cubed
chopped fresh parsley, for serving

1 Remove the tentacles from the calamari and pull the quill away. Discard the skin. Wash the tubes thoroughly and cut them into rings.
2 Scrub the mussels and remove the beards. Discard any open mussels. Put the mussels in a large pan with the wine and half the onion, cover and bring to the boil. Reduce the heat and simmer for 5 minutes. Discard any unopened ones. Set aside, reserving the wine and onion mixture.
3 Heat the oil in a large frying pan, add the chicken and cook for 5 minutes, or until golden. Remove and set aside.

4 Add the remaining onion to the pan with the garlic and capsicum. Cook, stirring often, for 5 minutes. Add the tomato, peas and cabanossi, stir to combine and season with the cayenne, salt and black pepper. Add the rice, stir to combine, then pour in the reserved wine and onion mixture. Stir the saffron into the stock to dissolve, then add to the pan.
5 Bring the mixture slowly to the boil, reduce the heat to low and

simmer, uncovered, for 15 minutes. Place the calamari rings, fish and chicken on top of the rice, then cover and cook for another 10–15 minutes, or until the rice is tender. Add the cooked mussels and cover to heat through. Sprinkle with fresh parsley and serve.

NUTRITION PER SERVE
Protein 25 g; Fat 3.5 g; Carbohydrate 20 g; Dietary Fibre 3.5 g; Cholesterol 115 mg; 975 kJ (235 cal)

Pull the tentacles and quill away from the body of the calamari.

Pull the skin off the calamari and discard it. Wash the tubes thoroughly.

Cook the mussels in the wine, with half the onion. Discard any unopened mussels.

SMOKED SALMON PIZZAS

Fat per serve: 8 g
Preparation time: 20 minutes
Total cooking time: 15 minutes
Serves 6

250 g (8 oz) ricotta
6 small oval pitta breads
125 g (4 oz) sliced smoked
salmon

1 small red onion, sliced
1 tablespoon baby capers
small dill sprigs, to garnish
1 lemon, cut into thin wedges,
for serving

1 Preheat the oven to moderate 180°C (350°F/Gas 4). Put the ricotta in a bowl, season well with salt and freshly cracked pepper, and stir until smooth. Spread the ricotta over the breads, leaving a border.

2 Top each pizza with some smoked salmon slices, then some onion pieces. Scatter baby capers over the top and bake on a baking tray for 15 minutes, or until the bases are slightly crispy around the edges. Garnish with a few dill sprigs and serve with lemon wedges.

NUTRITION PER SERVE
Protein 20 g; Fat 8 g; Carbohydrate 60 g; Dietary Fibre 4 g; Cholesterol 30 mg; 1650 kJ (395 cal)

Peel the red onion and then cut it into thin slices.

Spread the seasoned ricotta over the pitta breads, leaving a border.

Put some smoked salmon slices over the ricotta, followed by onion and capers.

VITAL VEGETABLES

MUSHROOM, RICOTTA AND OLIVE PIZZA

Fat per serve: 7.5 g
Preparation time: 30 minutes + proving
Total cooking time: 1 hour
Serves 6

4 Roma tomatoes, quartered
3/4 teaspoon caster sugar
7 g (1/4 oz) dry yeast or
    15 g (1/2 oz) fresh
1/2 cup (125 ml/4 fl oz) skim
    milk
13/4 cups (220 g/7 oz) plain flour
2 teaspoons olive oil
2 cloves garlic, crushed
1 onion, thinly sliced
750 g (11/2 lb) cap mushrooms,
    sliced
1 cup (250 g/8 oz) ricotta
2 tablespoons sliced black olives
small fresh basil leaves

1 Preheat the oven to hot 210°C (415°F/Gas 6–7). Put the tomato on a baking tray covered with baking paper, sprinkle with salt, cracked black pepper and 1/2 teaspoon sugar and bake for 20 minutes, or until the edges are starting to darken.

2 Stir the yeast and remaining sugar with 3 tablespoons warm water until the yeast dissolves. Cover and leave in a warm place until foamy. Warm the milk. Sift the flour into a large bowl and stir in the yeast and milk. Mix to a soft dough, then turn onto a lightly floured surface and knead for 5 minutes. Leave, covered, in a lightly oiled bowl in a warm place for 40 minutes, or until doubled in size.

3 Heat the oil in a pan and fry the garlic and onion until soft. Add the mushrooms and stir until they are soft and the liquid has evaporated. Cool.

4 Turn the dough out onto a lightly floured surface and knead lightly. Roll out to a 36 cm (15 inch) circle and transfer to a lightly greased oven or pizza tray. Spread with the ricotta, leaving a border to turn over the filling. Top with the mushrooms, leaving a circle in the centre and arrange the tomato and olives in the circle. Fold the dough edge over onto the mushroom and dust the edge with flour. Bake for 25 minutes, or until the crust is golden. Garnish with basil.

NUTRITION PER SERVE
Protein 15 g; Fat 7.5 g; Carbohydrate 30g; Dietary Fibre 6 g; Cholesterol 20 mg; 1100 kJ (265 cal)

The yeast mixture is ready when it has a foamy appearance.

Spread the ricotta over the pastry, leaving a border to turn over the filling.

LAYERED COUNTRY COB

Fat per serve: 9 g
Preparation time: 40 minutes
  + overnight refrigeration
Total cooking time: 25 minutes
Serves 8

2 red capsicums
1 eggplant, thinly sliced
1 large red onion, thinly sliced
450 g (14 oz) white cob loaf
1 tablespoon olive oil
2 cloves garlic, finely chopped
1 teaspoon chopped fresh lemon
    thyme
250 g (8 oz) English spinach
350 g (12 oz) ricotta

1 Preheat the grill to hot. Cut the capsicums in half lengthways and remove the seeds and membrane. Arrange the capsicum, skin-side-up, and the eggplant, sprayed lightly with oil, on the grill. Grill for about 7 minutes, turning the eggplant over as it browns, until the capsicum skin is blackened and blistered; cool. Grill the onion for about 6 minutes, turning once, until softened. Peel the capsicum.
2 Cut the top off the cob and pull out the centre. Combine the oil, garlic and thyme and brush lightly inside the shell. Put the spinach leaves in a bowl and pour boiling water over, to cover. Allow to soften for 1 minute, rinse with cold water until cool, then drain and pat dry with paper towels.
3 To fill the cob, arrange half the eggplant in the base, followed by capsicum and onion, then a layer of ricotta, spinach and the remaining eggplant. Season between layers. Press down firmly. If the top of the cob is empty, fill the space with a little of the soft bread from the centre. Replace the top and wrap securely with foil. Top with a brick wrapped in foil, or a heavy bowl. Refrigerate overnight. Cut into wedges to serve.

NUTRITION PER SERVE
Protein 10 g; Fat 9 g; Carbohydrate 30 g; Dietary Fibre 4 g; Cholesterol 20 mg; 1040 kJ (250 cal)

Cut the top off the cob loaf and pull the bread from the centre.

Put half the eggplant in the cob, then capsicum and onion.

Wrap the cob in foil and top with a brick wrapped in foil, or a heavy bowl.

RED LENTIL AND RICOTTA LASAGNE

Fat per serve: 10 g
Preparation time: 30 minutes + soaking
Total cooking time: 2 hours 10 minutes
Serves 6

½ cup (125 g/4 oz) red lentils
2 teaspoons olive oil
2–3 cloves garlic, crushed
1 large onion, chopped
1 small red capsicum, chopped
2 zucchini, sliced
1 celery stick, sliced
2 x 425 g (14 oz) cans chopped
    tomatoes
2 tablespoons tomato paste
1 teaspoon dried oregano
350 g (12 oz) ricotta
12 instant or fresh lasagne sheets
60 g (2 oz) reduced-fat cheese,
    grated

White sauce
⅓ cup (40 g/1¼ oz) cornflour
3 cups (750 ml/24 fl oz) skim
    milk
¼ onion
½ teaspoon ground nutmeg
freshly ground black pepper

1 Soak the lentils in boiling water to cover, for at least 30 minutes, then drain. Meanwhile, heat the oil in a large pan, add the garlic and onion and cook for 2 minutes. Add the capsicum, zucchini and celery and cook for 2–3 minutes.

2 Add the lentils, tomato, tomato paste, oregano and 1½ cups (375 ml/ 12 fl oz) water. Bring slowly to the boil, reduce the heat and simmer for 30 minutes, or until the lentils are tender. Stir occasionally.

3 To make the white sauce, blend the cornflour with 2 tablespoons of the milk until smooth. Pour the remaining milk into the pan, add the onion and stir over low heat until the mixture boils and thickens. Add the nutmeg and pepper, then cook over low heat for 5 minutes. Remove the onion.

4 Beat the ricotta with about ½ cup (125 ml/4 fl oz) of the white sauce. Preheat the oven to moderate 180°C (350°F/Gas 4). Spread one-third of the lentil mixture over the base of a 3-litre capacity ovenproof dish. Cover with a layer of lasagne sheets. Spread another third of the lentil mixture over the pasta, then spread the ricotta evenly over the top. Follow with another layer of lasagne, then the remaining lentils. Pour the white sauce evenly over the top and sprinkle with the grated cheese. Bake for 1 hour, covering loosely with foil if the top starts to brown too much. Leave for 5 minutes before cutting for serving.

NUTRITION PER SERVE
Protein 25 g; Fat 10 g; Carbohydrate 65 g; Dietary Fibre 9 g; Cholesterol 40 mg; 1995 kJ (475 cal)

Chop the onion and capsicum into quite small pieces and slice the zucchini.

Cover the lentil mixture with a layer of lasagne sheets.

The white sauce is poured over the top of the lasagne.

Clockwise, from top left: Berry dressing; Walnut vinaigrette; Hummus dressing; Tomato sauce; Sweet ricotta cream; Roasted capsicum sauce; Herb, garlic and yoghurt.

Dressings

These delicious low-fat dressings will add another dimension to your meals.
Not only are they easy to make, but they are healthy as well.

HERB, GARLIC AND YOGHURT

Whisk together 200 g (6½ oz) low-fat natural yoghurt, 4 tablespoons low-fat milk, 1 teaspoon Dijon mustard, 1 tablespoon finely chopped chives, 2 teaspoons finely chopped fresh parsley, 2 teaspoons chopped fresh oregano and 1 crushed clove garlic. Season. Makes 1 cup (250 ml/8 fl oz).

NUTRITION PER TABLESPOON
Protein 1 g; Fat 0 g; Carbohydrate 1 g; Dietary Fibre 0 g; Cholesterol 1 mg; 50 kJ (10 cal)

BERRY DRESSING

Blend 100 g (3½ oz) fresh or thawed frozen strawberries, 1½ tablespoons oil, ¼ cup (60 ml/2 fl oz) apple juice, 1 tablespoon fresh lemon juice, 1 tablespoon cider vinegar and some cracked black pepper, in a blender, until smooth. Season with salt. Makes ¾ cup (185 ml/6 fl oz).

NUTRITION PER TABLESPOON
Protein 0 g; Fat 3 g; Carbohydrate 1 g; Dietary Fibre 0 g; Cholesterol 0 mg; 145 kJ (35 cal)

WALNUT VINAIGRETTE

Combine 2 tablespoons cider vinegar, 1 tablespoon balsamic vinegar, 1½ tablespoons walnut oil, 1 teaspoon Dijon mustard, 2 tablespoons water, ½ teaspoon caster sugar and 2 teaspoons finely chopped fresh parsley in a screw-topped jar. Shake the jar, then season. Makes ½ cup (125 ml/4 fl oz).

NUTRITION PER TABLESPOON
Protein 0 g; Fat 5 g; Carbohydrate 1 g; Dietary Fibre 0 g; Cholesterol 0 mg; 210 kJ (50 cal)

ROASTED CAPSICUM SAUCE

Quarter 2 red capsicums, remove the seeds and membrane and grill until the skins blister and blacken. Cool under a damp tea towel before peeling. Cut one quarter into thin strips; set aside. Heat 1 teaspoon oil in a small pan, add 2 finely chopped spring onions and 1 tablespoon water, then stir over heat until the spring onion is soft. Add the remaining capsicum, 1/4 cup (60 ml/2 fl oz) beef stock, 2 tablespoons white wine, 2 tablespoons tomato paste and 1/4 teaspoon sugar. Simmer 2 minutes, then blend until smooth. Season and stir in 1 tablespoon chopped chives. Garnish with red capsicum strips. Makes 1 cup (250 ml/8 fl oz).

NUTRITION PER TABLESPOON
Protein 0.5 g; Fat 0.5 g; Carbohydrate 1.5 g; Dietary Fibre 0.5 g; Cholesterol 0 mg; 55 kJ (15 cal)

TOMATO SAUCE

Heat 1 teaspoon oil in a pan, add a sliced small leek (white part only), 2 tablespoons water and 1 crushed clove garlic. Cover and stir until the leek is soft. Add a 440 g (14 oz) can undrained chopped tomato, 1 tablespoon tomato paste, 1/4 teaspoon sugar and 2 tablespoons red wine. Stir, then simmer for 5 minutes. Season. Makes 2 cups (500 ml/16 fl oz).

NUTRITION PER TABLESPOON
Protein 0.5 g; Fat 0.5 g; Carbohydrate 1.5 g; Dietary Fibre 0.5 g; Cholesterol 0 mg; 55 kJ (15 cal)

HUMMUS DRESSING

Drain a 425 g (14 oz) can chickpeas and put in a food processor with 3/4 cup (185 ml/6 fl oz) vegetable stock, 1 tablespoon tahini paste and 2 chopped cloves garlic. Stir 1 teaspoon each of ground coriander and cumin in a dry frying pan over medium heat for 3 minutes, or until aromatic. Cool slightly, add to the processor and mix until nearly smooth. Mix in 2 tablespoons lemon juice. Season with freshly cracked pepper and salt. If too thick, add a little water. Makes 1 cup (250 ml/8 fl oz).

NUTRITION PER TABLESPOON
Protein 2 g; Fat 1.5 g; Carbohydrate 4 g; Dietary Fibre 1.5 g; Cholesterol 0 mg; 160 kJ (40 cal)

SWEET RICOTTA CREAM

Beat together 200 g (6 1/2 oz) ricotta, 100 g (3 1/2 oz) low-fat natural yoghurt, 1/2 teaspoon finely grated orange rind, 3 tablespoons orange juice and 1 tablespoon caster sugar until smooth. Makes 1 cup (250 ml/8 fl oz).

NUTRITION PER TABLESPOON
Protein 2 g; Fat 1.5 g; Carbohydrate 2.5 g; Dietary Fibre 0 g; Cholesterol 6.5 mg; 130 kJ (30 cal)

FRITTATA

Fat per serve: 5 g
Preparation time: 25 minutes
Total cooking time: 25 minutes
Serves 6

200 g (6½ oz) zucchini,
    cubed
250 g (8 oz) pumpkin, cubed
300 g (10 oz) potato, cubed
100 g (3½ oz) broccoli florets
3 teaspoons oil
1 small onion, chopped
1 small red capsicum, chopped

2 tablespoons finely chopped
    fresh parsley
3 eggs
2 egg whites

1 Steam the zucchini, pumpkin, potato and broccoli until tender, then transfer to a bowl.

2 Heat 2 teaspoons of the oil in a non-stick frying pan, about 22 cm (9 inch) diameter. Add the onion and capsicum and cook for 3 minutes, or until tender. Mix with the steamed vegetables, along with the parsley.

3 Brush the pan with the remaining oil. Return all the vegetables to the pan and spread out with a spatula to an even thickness. Beat the eggs and whites together and pour into the pan, tilting to distribute evenly.

4 Cook over medium heat until the eggs are almost set, but still runny on top. Wrap the handle of the pan in a damp tea towel to protect it and place the pan under the grill to cook the frittata top (pierce gently with a fork to make sure it is cooked through). Cut into wedges and serve.

NUTRITION PER SERVE
Protein 8 g; Fat 5 g; Carbohydrate 10 g;
Dietary Fibre 3 g; Cholesterol 90 mg;
515 kJ (125 cal)

Stir the finely chopped onion and capsicum until tender.

Beat the combined eggs and whites and pour into the pan over the vegetables.

The eggs should be almost set, but still runny on top, before grilling to brown.

VEGETABLE CURRY

Fat per serve: 4 g
Preparation time: 30 minutes
Total cooking time: 45 minutes
Serves 6

2 teaspoons olive oil
1 onion, chopped
2 cloves garlic, crushed
2 teaspoons ground cumin
2 teaspoons ground coriander
3 teaspoons Madras curry powder
500 g (1 lb) potatoes, cut into
    bite-sized pieces
500 g (1 lb) pumpkin, cut into
    bite-sized pieces

2 large zucchini, thickly sliced
2 large carrots, thickly sliced
400 g (13 oz) can chopped
    tomatoes
1 cup (250 ml/8 fl oz) vegetable
    stock
100 g (3½ oz) broccoli florets
150 g (5 oz) green beans, cut
    into short lengths
¼ cup (15 g/½ oz) chopped
    fresh coriander
1 cup (250 g/8 oz) low-fat
    natural yoghurt

1 Heat the oil in a large deep pan, add the onion and garlic and cook until softened. Add the ground cumin, coriander and curry powder and cook

for 1–2 minutes, or until fragrant. Add the potato, pumpkin, zucchini and carrot and toss to coat in the spices.
2 Stir in the tomato and stock, bring to the boil, then reduce the heat and simmer, covered, for 30 minutes, or until the vegetables are tender, stirring frequently. Add the broccoli florets and chopped beans and simmer, uncovered, for 5 minutes, or until all the vegetables are tender. Stir in the chopped coriander and serve with yoghurt. Can be served with steamed rice.

NUTRITION PER SERVE
Protein 8.5 g; Fat 4 g; Carbohydrate 25 g;
Dietary Fibre 6 g; Cholesterol 7 mg;
715 kJ (170 cal)

Prepare the carrots and zucchini by cutting into thick slices.

Stir in the cumin, ground coriander and curry powder until aromatic.

When the vegetables are coated in spices, stir in the tomato and stock.

VEGETABLE STRUDEL PARCELS

Fat per serve: 8 g
Preparation time: about 1 hour
Total cooking time: 30 minutes
Serves 4

300 g (10 oz) pumpkin
2 carrots
1 parsnip
2 celery sticks
2 teaspoons sesame oil
1 onion, finely sliced
3 teaspoons finely chopped or
    grated ginger
1 tablespoon dry sherry
1 teaspoon finely grated lemon
    rind
1 cup (185 g/6 oz) cooked long-
    grain rice
2 tablespoons plum sauce
1 tablespoon sweet chilli sauce
2 teaspoons soy sauce
16 sheets filo pastry
1/3 cup (35 g/1 1/4 oz) dry
    breadcrumbs
1 teaspoon butter, melted
1 tablespoon sesame seeds
sweet chilli sauce, for serving

1 Cut the pumpkin, carrots, parsnip and celery into thick matchsticks about 2.5 mm (1/8 inch) wide and 5 cm (2 inches) long.
2 Heat the sesame oil in a heavy-based pan or wok, add the onion and ginger and stir-fry, tossing well until brown, over medium heat. Add the pumpkin, carrot and parsnip, toss well and cook for 1 minute. Sprinkle 2 teaspoons of water all over the vegetables, cover and steam for another minute. Add the celery, sherry and lemon rind, toss and cook for 1 minute. Cover again and let steam for about 1 minute, or until the vegetables are just tender. Stir in the cooked rice and the plum, chilli and soy sauces. Set aside for about 20 minutes to cool.
3 Preheat the oven to moderately hot 190°C (375°F/Gas 5). Remove two sheets of filo pastry, keeping the remaining pastry covered with a damp tea towel. Place one sheet on top of the other, carefully brush the edges lightly with a little water, then scatter some breadcrumbs over the pastry. Top with another 2 sheets of pastry, fold over the edges to make a 2 cm (3/4 inch) border and brush lightly with a little water. Press the edges down gently with your fingertips to make the parcel easier to fold.
4 Place one-quarter of the filling about 5 cm (2 inches) from the short end, then firmly roll into a parcel to encase the filling, ensuring that the seam is underneath. Repeat with the remaining ingredients.
5 Brush the tops very lightly with butter, cut 3 slashes across the top of each and scatter any remaining breadcrumbs and the sesame seeds over the top. Arrange on a lightly greased baking tray and bake for 20–25 minutes, or until crisp and golden. Serve immediately, drizzled with sweet chilli sauce.

NUTRITION PER SERVE
Protein 15 g; Fat 8 g; Carbohydrate 95 g; Dietary Fibre 7 g; Cholesterol 3 mg; 2210 kJ (530 cal)

COOK'S FILE

Hint: Cover the unused filo pastry with a damp tea towel to prevent it drying out.

Cut the pumpkin, carrot, parsnip and celery into similar-sized short matchsticks.

Stir the rice and plum, chilli and soy sauces into the vegetables.

Moisten the pastry before scattering the breadcrumbs over it.

Fold the edges over, brush with water, then press down lightly.

Put the filling on the pastry, then firmly roll into a parcel.

Cut 3 slashes on the top of each parcel to allow steam to escape.

ROAST VEGETABLE QUICHE

Fat per serve: 10 g
Preparation time: 45 minutes
  + 25 minutes refrigeration
Total cooking time: 2 hours 30 minutes
Serves 6

cooking oil spray
1 large potato
400 g (13 oz) pumpkin
200 g (6½ oz) orange sweet
    potato
2 large parsnips
1 red capsicum
2 onions, cut into wedges
6 cloves garlic, halved
2 teaspoons olive oil
1¼ cups (155 g/5 oz) plain flour
40 g (1¼ oz) butter
45 g (1½ oz) ricotta
1 cup (250 ml/8 fl oz) skim milk
3 eggs, lightly beaten
¼ cup (30 g/1 oz) reduced-fat
    Cheddar, grated
2 tablespoons chopped fresh basil

1 Preheat the oven to moderate 180°C (350°F/Gas 4). Lightly spray a 3.5 cm (1¼ inch) deep, 23 cm (9 inch) diameter loose-based flan tin with oil. Cut the potato, pumpkin, sweet potato, parsnips and capsicum into bite-sized chunks, place in a baking dish with the onion and garlic and drizzle with the oil. Season and bake for 1 hour, or until tender. Leave to cool.
2 Mix the flour, butter and ricotta in a food processor, then gradually add up to 3 tablespoons of the milk, enough to form a soft dough. Turn out onto a lightly floured surface and gather together into a smooth ball. Cover and refrigerate for 15 minutes.

3 Roll the pastry out on a lightly floured surface, then ease into the tin, bringing it gently up the side. Trim the edge and refrigerate for another 10 minutes. Increase the oven to moderately hot 200°C (400°F/Gas 6). Cover the pastry with crumpled baking paper and fill with baking beads or uncooked rice. Bake for 10 minutes, remove the beads or rice and paper, then bake for another 10 minutes, or until golden brown.

4 Place the vegetables in the pastry base and pour in the combined remaining milk, eggs, cheese and basil. Reduce the oven temperature to moderate 180°C (350°F/Gas 4) and bake for 1 hour 10 minutes, or until set in the centre. Leave for 5 minutes before removing from the tin to serve.

NUTRITION PER SERVE
Protein 15 g; Fat 10 g; Carbohydrate 45 g; Dietary Fibre 5.5 g; Cholesterol 115 mg; 1440 kJ (345 cal)

Put the vegetables in a baking dish and drizzle with the olive oil.

Ease the pastry into the flan tin, bring it up the side, then trim the edge.

Mix the milk, eggs, cheese and basil and pour over the vegetables.

STUFFED EGGPLANTS

Fat per serve: 10 g
Preparation time: 20 minutes
Total cooking time: 1 hour
Serves 4

^{1}/3 cup (60 g/2 oz) brown lentils
2 large eggplants
cooking oil spray
1 red onion, chopped
2 cloves garlic, crushed
1 red capsicum, finely chopped
^{1}/4 cup (40 g/1^1/4 oz) pine nuts,
   toasted
440 g (14 oz) can chopped
   tomatoes

^{3}/4 cup (140 g/4^1/2 oz) cooked
   short-grain rice
2 tablespoons chopped fresh
   coriander
1 tablespoon chopped fresh
   parsley
2 tablespoons grated Parmesan

1 Simmer the brown lentils in a pan of water for 25 minutes, or until soft; drain. Slice the eggplants in half lengthways and scoop out the flesh, leaving a 1 cm (^{1}/2 inch) shell. Chop the flesh finely.

2 Spray a deep, large non-stick frying pan with oil, add 1 tablespoon water to the pan, then add the onion and garlic and stir until softened. Add the cooked lentils to the pan with the capsicum, pine nuts, tomato, rice and eggplant flesh. Stir over medium heat for 10 minutes, or until the eggplant has softened. Add the fresh coriander and parsley. Season, then toss until well mixed.

3 Cook the eggplant shells in boiling water for 4–5 minutes, or until tender, or microwave on High (100%) for 8 minutes. Spoon the filling into the eggplant shells and sprinkle with the Parmesan. Grill for 5–10 minutes, or until golden. Serve immediately.

NUTRITION PER SERVE
Protein 15 g; Fat 10 g; Carbohydrate 50 g; Dietary Fibre 8.5 g; Cholesterol 9.5 mg; 1490 kJ (355 cal)

Scoop out the flesh, leaving a shell on the inside of the eggplant halves.

Stir in the chopped fresh coriander and parsley and season.

Cook the eggplant halves for about 5 minutes, until tender.

SILVERBEET PARCELS

Fat per serve: 6 g
Preparation time: 40 minutes
Total cooking time: 1 hour
Serves 6

2 cups (500 ml/16 fl oz)
    vegetable stock
1 tablespoon olive oil
1 onion, chopped
2 cloves garlic, crushed
1 red capsicum, chopped
250 g (8 oz) mushrooms, chopped
1/2 cup (110 g/3½ oz) arborio
    rice
60 g (2 oz) reduced-fat Cheddar,
    grated
1/4 cup (15 g/1/2 oz) shredded
    fresh basil
6 large silverbeet leaves
2 x 400 g (13 oz) cans chopped
    tomatoes
1 tablespoon balsamic vinegar
1 teaspoon soft brown sugar

1 Heat the vegetable stock in a pan and maintain at simmering point. Heat the oil in a large pan, add the onion and garlic and cook until the onion has softened. Add the capsicum, mushrooms and rice and stir until well combined. Gradually add 1/2 cup (125 ml/4 fl oz) hot stock, stirring until the liquid has been absorbed. Continue to add the stock, a little at a time, until it has all been absorbed and the rice is tender (this will take about 20 minutes). Remove from the heat, add the cheese and basil and season well.

2 Trim the stalks from the silverbeet and cook the leaves, a few at a time, in a large pan of boiling water for 30 seconds, or until wilted. Drain on a tea towel. Using a sharp knife, cut away any tough white veins from the centre of the leaves without cutting them in half. If necessary, overlap the 2 sides to make a flat surface. Place a portion of mushroom filling in the centre of each leaf, fold in the sides and roll up carefully. Tie with string.

3 Put the tomato, balsamic vinegar and sugar in a large, deep non-stick frying pan and stir to combine. Add the silverbeet parcels, cover and simmer for 10 minutes. Remove the string and serve with tomato sauce.

NUTRITION PER SERVE
Protein 7.5 g; Fat 6 g; Carbohydrate 20 g;
Dietary Fibre 4 g; Cholesterol 7 mg;
725 kJ (175 cal)

Add the stock, a little at a time, until the rice is tender and has absorbed the stock.

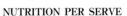

Using a sharp knife, cut away white veins from the centre of the leaves.

Place filling in the centre of each leaf, fold in the sides and roll up into parcels.

PUMPKIN AND BROAD BEAN RISOTTO

Fat per serve: 12 g
Preparation time: 35 minutes
Total cooking time: 50 minutes
Serves 4

350 g (12 oz) pumpkin
cooking oil spray
1 tablespoon olive oil
1 large onion, finely chopped
2 cloves garlic, finely chopped
1 cup (220 g/7 oz) arborio rice
3 cups (750 ml/24 fl oz)
   vegetable stock

200 g (6½ oz) swiss brown
   mushrooms, halved
2 cups (310 g/10 oz) frozen
   broad beans, defrosted, peeled
4 tablespoons grated Parmesan

1 Preheat the oven to moderately hot 200°C (400°F/Gas 6). Cut the pumpkin into small chunks and spray lightly with oil, on a baking tray. Bake, turning occasionally, for 20 minutes, or until tender. Set aside, covered.
2 Meanwhile, heat the oil in a large heavy-based pan, add the onion and garlic, cover and cook for 10 minutes over low heat. Put the stock in a pan and keep at simmering point.

3 Add the rice to the onion and stir for 2 minutes. Gradually stir in ½ cup (125 ml/4 fl oz) of the hot stock, until absorbed. Stir in another ½ cup (125 ml/4 fl oz) of hot stock until absorbed. Add the mushrooms and continue adding the remaining stock, a little at a time, until it is all absorbed and the rice is just tender (this will take about 20 minutes).
4 Stir in the cooked pumpkin and the broad beans. Sprinkle with the grated Parmesan.

NUTRITION PER SERVE
Protein 20 g; Fat 12 g; Carbohydrate 60 g; Dietary Fibre 10 g; Cholesterol 20 mg; 1775 kJ (425 cal)

Put the chunks of pumpkin on a baking tray and spray with oil.

Add the stock to the rice, a little at a time, and stir until dissolved.

Add the mushrooms, then continue stirring in the stock until absorbed.

SPINACH PIE

Fat per serve: 10 g
Preparation time: 25 minutes
Total cooking time: 45 minutes
Serves 6

1.5 kg (3 lb) English spinach
2 teaspoons olive oil
1 onion, chopped
4 spring onions, chopped
750 g (1 1/2 lb) reduced-fat
    cottage cheese
2 eggs, lightly beaten
2 cloves garlic, crushed
pinch of ground nutmeg
1/4 cup (15 g/1/2 oz) chopped
    fresh mint
8 sheets filo pastry
30 g (1 oz) butter, melted
1/2 cup (40 g/1 1/4 oz) fresh
    breadcrumbs

1 Preheat the oven to moderate 180°C (350°F/Gas 4). Lightly spray a square 1.5 litre capacity ovenproof dish with oil. Trim and wash the spinach, then place in a large pan. Cover and cook for 2–3 minutes, until the spinach is just wilted. Drain, cool then squeeze dry and chop.

2 Heat the oil in a small pan. Add the onion and spring onion and cook for 2–3 minutes, until softened. Combine in a bowl with the chopped spinach. Stir in the cottage cheese, egg, garlic, nutmeg and mint. Season and mix thoroughly.

3 Brush a sheet of filo pastry with a little butter. Fold in half widthways and line the base and sides of the dish. Repeat with 3 more sheets. Keep the unused sheets moist by covering with a damp tea towel.

4 Sprinkle the breadcrumbs over the

pastry. Spread the filling into the dish. Fold over any overlapping pastry. Brush and fold another sheet and place on top. Repeat with 3 more sheets. Tuck the pastry in at the sides. Brush the top with any remaining butter. Score squares or

diamonds on top using a sharp knife. Bake for 40 minutes, or until golden. Cut into squares to serve.

NUTRITION PER SERVE
Protein 35 g; Fat 10 g; Carbohydrate 30 g; Dietary Fibre 8 g; Cholesterol 75 mg; 1500 kJ (360 cal)

Squeeze any excess moisture out of the cooled spinach.

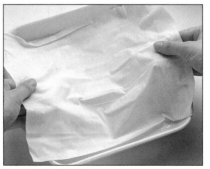

Line the base and sides of the dish with the greased and folded filo.

When you have lined the top with pastry, tuck it in at the sides.

PASTA WITH ROASTED TOMATO SAUCE

Fat per serve: 3.5 g
Preparation time: 25 minutes
Total cooking time: 50 minutes
Serves 4

1 kg (2 lb) ripe Roma tomatoes
8 cloves garlic, unpeeled
2 tablespoons olive oil
2 teaspoons dried basil
1 cup (250 ml/8 fl oz) vegetable
 stock
½ cup (125 ml/4 fl oz) dry
 white wine
2 tablespoons balsamic vinegar
500 g (1 lb) tagliatelle
2 tablespoons grated Parmesan

1 Preheat the oven to moderate 180°C (350°F/Gas 4). Cut the tomatoes in half lengthways and arrange, cut-side-up, in the base of a baking dish. Sprinkle with 1 tablespoon water to prevent the tomatoes catching. Add the garlic to the pan and drizzle or brush the oil over the tomatoes and garlic. Sprinkle with basil, salt and freshly ground black pepper. Bake for 25 minutes, or until soft, and gently remove from the pan.
2 Heat the baking dish over low heat and add the stock, white wine and vinegar. Bring to the boil, reduce the heat and simmer for 20 minutes. Roughly chop the tomatoes, retaining all the juices. Squeeze the garlic out of the skin and add the tomato and garlic to the simmering sauce. Taste and adjust the seasonings.
3 Cook the pasta in a large pan of rapidly boiling salted water for about 10 minutes, or until *al dente*. Drain and keep warm. Serve the sauce over the pasta and sprinkle with Parmesan.

NUTRITION PER SERVE
Protein 20 g; Fat 3.5 g; Carbohydrate 95 g; Dietary Fibre 10 g; Cholesterol 5 mg; 2060 kJ (515 cal)

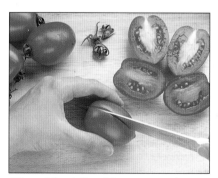

Discard the stalks of the tomatoes, then cut in half lengthways.

Add the stock, wine and vinegar to the baking dish and bring to the boil.

Squeeze the cooked garlic out of the skins and add to the sauce.

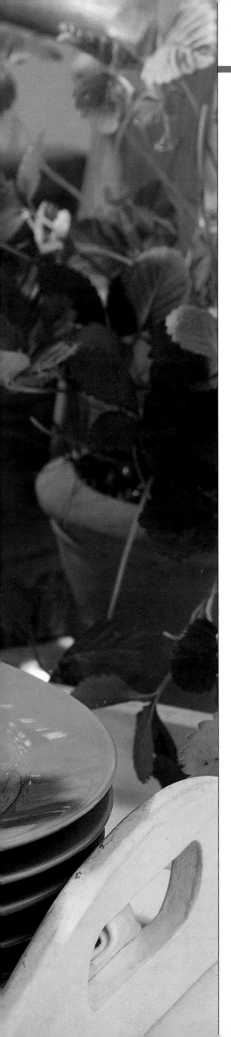

DESSERTS & BAKING

LEMON BERRY CHEESECAKE

Fat per serve: 6 g
Preparation time: 25 minutes
  + overnight refrigeration
Total cooking time: Nil
Serves 12

60 g (2 oz) plain un-iced
    biscuits, finely crushed
30 g (1 oz) butter, melted
300 g (10 oz) ricotta
2 tablespoons caster sugar
2 x 130 g (4¼ oz) tubs light
    French Vanilla Fruche or
    low-fat fromage frais
2 x 130 g (4½ oz) tubs light
    Lemon Tang Fruche or
    low-fat fromage frais
2 teaspoons finely grated lemon
    rind
2 tablespoons fresh lemon juice
1 tablespoon gelatine
2 egg whites
250 g (8 oz) strawberries, halved

1 Lightly oil and line the base and sides of a 20 cm (8 inch) diameter springform tin with plastic wrap. Combine the biscuit crumbs and butter in a small bowl and press evenly over the base of the tin. Refrigerate while making the filling.
2 Combine the ricotta and sugar in a food processor until smooth. Add all the fruche, the lemon rind and juice, then mix well. Put ¼ cup (60 ml/ 2 fl oz) water in a small bowl, sprinkle the gelatine in an even layer onto the surface and leave to go spongy. Bring a small pan of water to the boil, remove from the heat and put the gelatine bowl in the pan. The water should come halfway up the side of the bowl. Stir the gelatine until clear and dissolved, then cool slightly. Stir the gelatine mixture into the ricotta mixture, then transfer to a large bowl. Beat the egg whites until soft peaks form, then gently fold into the ricotta mixture.
3 Pour the mixture into the prepared tin and refrigerate for several hours or overnight, until set. Carefully remove from the tin by removing the side of the pan and gently easing the plastic from underneath. Decorate with the halved strawberries.

NUTRITION PER SERVE
Protein 5 g; Fat 6 g; Carbohydrate 8 g;
Dietary Fibre 1 g; Cholesterol 15 mg;
425 kJ (100 cal)

Combine the biscuit crumbs and butter, then press evenly over the base of the tin.

Gently fold the beaten egg white into the ricotta mixture.

FUDGE BROWNIES

Fat per serve: 3.5 g
Preparation time: 15 minutes
Total cooking time: 30 minutes
Makes 18

cooking oil spray
1/2 cup (60 g/2 oz) plain flour
1/2 cup (60 g/2 oz) self-raising
    flour
1 teaspoon bicarbonate of soda
3/4 cup (90 g/3 oz) cocoa
    powder
2 eggs

1 1/4 cups (310 g/10 oz) caster
    sugar
2 teaspoons vanilla essence
2 tablespoons vegetable oil
200 g (6 1/2 oz) Vanilla Fruche
    (1% fat) or low-fat fromage
    fraiche
140 ml (4 1/2 fl oz) apple purée
icing sugar, for dusting

1 Preheat the oven to moderate 180°C
(350°F/Gas 4). Spray a 30 x 20 cm
(12 x 8 inch) shallow baking tin with oil
and line the base with baking paper.
2 Sift the flours, bicarbonate of soda
and cocoa powder into a large bowl.

Mix the eggs, sugar, vanilla essence, oil,
fruche and purée in a large bowl,
stirring until well combined. Add to the
flour and stir until combined. Spread
into the prepared tin and bake for about
30 minutes, or until a skewer inserted
in the centre comes out clean.
3 The brownie will sink slightly in the
centre as it cools. Leave in the pan for
5 minutes before turning onto a wire
rack to cool. Dust with icing sugar
before cutting into pieces to serve.

NUTRITION PER SERVE
Protein 2.5 g; Fat 3.5 g; Carbohydrate 2.5 g;
Dietary Fibre 5 g; Cholesterol 20 mg;
595 kJ (140 cal)

Stir together the eggs, sugar, vanilla essence, oil, fruche and apple purée.

Add the egg mixture to the flour and stir thoroughly until combined.

Test with a skewer. When the brownie is cooked, the skewer will come out clean.

RHUBARB AND PEAR CRUMBLE

Fat per serve: 8 g
Preparation time: 20 minutes
Total cooking time: 35 minutes
Serves 6

600 g (1¼ lb) rhubarb
2 strips lemon rind
1 tablespoon honey, or to taste
2 firm, ripe pears
½ cup (50 g/1¾ oz) rolled oats
¼ cup (35 g/1¼ oz) wholemeal plain flour
⅓ cup (60 g/2 oz) soft brown sugar
50 g (1¾ oz) butter

1 Trim the rhubarb, wash and cut into 3 cm (1¼ inch) pieces. Place in a medium pan with the lemon rind and 1 tablespoon water. Cook, covered, over low heat for 10 minutes, or until tender. Cool a little. Stir in the honey and remove the lemon rind.

2 Preheat the oven to moderate 180°C (350°F/Gas 4). Peel, core and cut the pears into 2 cm (¾ inch) cubes and combine with the rhubarb. Pour into a 1.25 litre dish and smooth the surface.

3 To make the topping, combine the oats, flour and brown sugar in a bowl. Rub in the butter with your fingertips until the mixture is crumbly. Spread over the fruit. Bake for 15 minutes, or until cooked and golden.

NUTRITION PER SERVE
Protein 3.5 g; Fat 8 g; Carbohydrate 30 g; Dietary Fibre 6 g; Cholesterol 0 mg; 885 kJ (210 cal)

Trim the rhubarb, wash thoroughly, then cut into short pieces.

Add the cubed pears to the cooked rhubarb and gently stir to combine.

Use your fingertips to rub the butter into the dry ingredients.

PEARS POACHED IN DARK GRAPE JUICE

Fat per serve: Nil
Preparation time: 10–15 minutes
  + overnight refrigeration
Total cooking time: 1 hour 20 minutes
Serves 6

6 beurre bosc (or any firm) pears
2 tablespoons lemon juice
2 cups (500 ml/8 fl oz) dark
    grape juice
2 cups (500 ml/8 fl oz)
    blackcurrant juice
2 tablespoons sweet sherry
4 cloves
350 g (12 oz) black grapes
1 cup (250 g/8 oz) low-fat
    natural yoghurt
1/2 teaspoon ground cinnamon
1 tablespoon honey

1 Core and peel the pears, leaving the stalks on. Place the pears, as you peel, in a bowl filled with cold water and the lemon juice, to prevent browning.
2 Put the grape and blackcurrant juices, sherry and cloves in a saucepan large enough to hold the pears. (The size of the saucepan will depend on the size of the pears.)
3 Bring the liquid to the boil, then reduce to a simmer. Cover and cook for 35–40 minutes, or until tender. Remove from the heat and leave the pears to cool in the syrup. Transfer the pears and syrup to a bowl and cover with plastic wrap. Refrigerate overnight.
4 To serve, strain the syrup into a pan, bring to the boil, then reduce to a simmer and cook for 40 minutes, or until reduced by about two-thirds. Cool slightly, place a pear on each plate and pour syrup over the pears.

Arrange the grapes next to the pears. Just before serving, mix the yoghurt, cinnamon and honey and spoon over the pears or serve on the side.

NUTRITION PER SERVE
Protein 4 g; Fat 0 g; Carbohydrate 95 g; Dietary Fibre 4 g; Cholesterol 2 mg; 1630 kJ (390 cal)

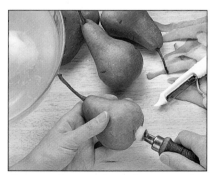

Remove the core from the pears, then peel, leaving the stalks on.

Bring the liquid to the boil, then reduce the heat and simmer until tender.

Mix the yoghurt, cinnamon and honey just before serving the pears.

FRUIT TARTS

Fat per serve: 8 g
Preparation time: 25 minutes
  + 30 minutes refrigeration
Total cooking time: 20 minutes
Makes 8

1 cup (125 g/4 oz) plain flour
1/4 cup (30 g/1 oz) custard
    powder
1/4 cup (30 g/1 oz) icing sugar
40 g (1¼ oz) butter
2 tablespoons low-fat milk
2 x 130 g (4½ oz) tubs light
    Strawberry Fruche or
    low-fat fromage frais
100 g (3½ oz) ricotta
strawberries, blueberries,
    kiwi fruit
110 g (3½ oz) jar apple baby gel

1 Lightly grease eight 7 cm (2¾ inch) loose-based flan tins. Process the flour, custard powder, icing sugar and butter in a food processor until mixture forms fine crumbs, then add enough of the milk to form a soft dough. Gather together into a ball. Wrap in plastic and refrigerate for 30 minutes.

2 Preheat the oven to moderately hot 200°C (400°F/Gas 6). Divide the dough into 8 portions and roll each to fit the bases and sides of the prepared tins. Cover the pastry with paper and fill with uncooked rice or beans. Bake for 10 minutes, remove the rice or beans and paper and bake for another 10 minutes, or until golden. Allow to cool before removing from the tins.

3 Mix the fruche and ricotta until smooth. Spread over the pastry bases and top decoratively with assorted fruit. Bring a small pan of water to the boil, remove from heat. Put the baby gel in a small bowl and put the bowl in the water. Stir until melted. Brush over the fruit and refrigerate until set.

NUTRITION PER SERVE
Protein 3.5 g; Fat 8 g; Carbohydrate 20 g; Dietary Fibre 1 g; Cholesterol 20 mg; 690 kJ (165 cal)

Add enough milk to the crumbly mixture to form a soft dough.

Cover the pastry with baking paper and fill with uncooked rice or beans.

Remove the rice or beans and paper and return the pastry to the oven until golden.

MERINGUE BASKETS WITH GLAZED FRUITS

Fat per serve: 0.5 g
Preparation time: 40 minutes + cooling
Total cooking time: 1 hour 30 minutes
Serves 6

2 egg whites
small pinch cream of tartar
1/2 cup (125 g/4 oz) caster sugar
2 tablespoons custard powder
2 cups (500 ml/16 fl oz) skim
  milk
1 teaspoon vanilla essence
1 peach, cut into thin wedges
1 kiwi fruit, cut into thin wedges
2 strawberries, halved
110 g (3 1/2 oz) jar apple baby gel

1 Preheat the oven to slow 150°C (300°F/Gas 2) and line a baking tray with baking paper. Beat the egg whites and cream of tartar with electric beaters until soft peaks form. Gradually add the sugar and beat until it is dissolved and the mixture is stiff and glossy.

2 Fit a piping bag with a medium star nozzle and pipe coiled spirals of the meringue (about 8 cm/3 inches) onto the tray. Pipe an extra ring around the top edge to make baskets. Bake for 30 minutes, then reduce the heat to very slow 120°C (250°F/Gas 1/2). Bake for 45 minutes, turn the oven off and cool with the oven door ajar.

3 Mix the custard powder with a little of the milk to form a smooth paste. Transfer to a pan with the remaining milk and the vanilla essence. Stir over medium heat until the mixture boils and thickens. Remove from the heat and place plastic wrap over the surface to stop a skin forming. Set aside and, when cool, stir until smooth.

Spoon some of the cold custard into each basket. Top with fruit. In a saucepan, heat the gel until runny and brush lightly over the fruits.

NUTRITION PER SERVE
Protein 5 g; Fat 0.5 g; Carbohydrate 30 g; Dietary Fibre 1 g; Cholesterol 3 mg; 590 kJ (140 cal)

Beat the egg whites and cream of tartar until soft peaks form.

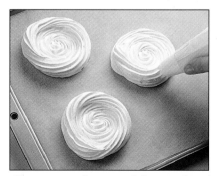

Pipe an extra ring around the top edge of the coils to make baskets.

Put a layer of plastic wrap over the surface of the custard.

RASPBERRY MOUSSE

Fat per serve: 2 g
Preparation time: 30 minutes
 + refrigeration
Total cooking time: Nil
Serves 4

3 teaspoons gelatine
1 cup (250 g/8 oz) low-fat
 vanilla yoghurt
2 x 200 g (6½ oz) tubs French
 Vanilla Fruche or low-fat
 fromage frais
4 egg whites
150 g (5 oz) fresh or frozen,
 thawed, raspberries, mashed
fresh raspberries and mint
 leaves, for serving

1 Sprinkle the gelatine in an even layer onto 1 tablespoon water in a small bowl and leave to go spongy. Bring a small pan of water to the boil, remove from the heat and place the bowl in the pan. Stir until clear and dissolved.
2 In a large bowl, stir the vanilla yoghurt and fruche together, then add the gelatine and mix well.
3 Using electric beaters, beat the egg whites until stiff peaks form, then fold through the yoghurt mixture. Transfer half to a separate bowl and fold the mashed raspberries through.
4 Divide the raspberry mixture into the bases of 4 long glasses or serving bowls. Top with the vanilla mixture. Refrigerate for several hours, or until set. Decorate with fresh raspberries and mint leaves.

NUTRITION PER SERVE
Protein 9.5 g; Fat 2 g; Carbohydrate 10 g;
Dietary Fibre 2 g; Cholesterol 4 mg;
355 kJ (85 cal)

Mash the fresh or frozen raspberries in a bowl.

Stir the vanilla yoghurt and fruche together until combined.

Gently fold the mashed raspberries through half the yoghurt mixture.

STRAWBERRY AND BANANA ICE

Fat per serve: 3 g
Preparation time: 10 minutes + freezing
Total cooking time: Nil
Serves 4

300 g (10 oz) silken tofu, chopped
250 g (4 oz) strawberries, roughly chopped

2 ripe bananas, roughly chopped
1/4 cup (60 g/2 oz) caster sugar

1 Blend the silken tofu, strawberries, banana and caster sugar in a blender or food processor, until smooth.
2 Pour the mixture into a shallow cake tin and freeze until almost frozen. Break up roughly with a fork or a spoon, then transfer to a large bowl and beat until it has a smooth texture. Pour the mixture evenly into a

15 x 25 cm (6 x 10 inch) loaf tin, cover and freeze again, until quite firm.
3 Alternatively, freeze the blended mixture in an ice cream machine until thick and creamy, then store in a covered container in the freezer.
4 Transfer to the refrigerator for about 30 minutes before serving to allow the ice to soften slightly.

NUTRITION PER SERVE
Protein 7 g; Fat 3 g; Carbohydrate 30 g; Dietary Fibre 3 g; Cholesterol 0 mg; 710 kJ (170 cal)

Blend the tofu, strawberries, banana and caster sugar until smooth.

When partially frozen, use a fork or spoon to break up the mixture.

Transfer the chopped mixture to a bowl and beat until smooth.

PASSIONFRUIT BAVAROIS

Fat per serve: 2.5 g
Preparation time: 10 minutes + overnight refrigeration
Total cooking time: Nil
Serves 8

2 x 170 g (5 1/2 oz) cans passionfruit syrup
300 g (10 oz) silken tofu, chopped
600 ml (20 fl oz) buttermilk
2 tablespoons caster sugar
1 teaspoon vanilla essence
6 teaspoons gelatine

3/4 cup (185 ml/6 fl oz) passionfruit pulp
8 strawberries, halved, to garnish

1 Push the passionfruit in syrup through a sieve. Discard the seeds. Combine the strained syrup with the tofu, buttermilk, caster sugar and vanilla in a blender. Blend for 90 seconds on high, to mix thoroughly. Leave in the blender.
2 Put 1/3 cup (80 ml/2 3/4 fl oz) water in a small bowl and put the bowl in a slightly larger bowl of boiling water. Sprinkle the gelatine onto the water in the small bowl and stir until dissolved. Leave to cool.

3 Place eight 200 ml (6 1/2 fl oz) dariole moulds in a baking dish. Add the gelatine to the blender and mix on high for 1 minute. Pour into the moulds, cover the dish with plastic wrap and refrigerate overnight.
4 When ready to serve, carefully run a spatula around the edge of each mould and dip the bases into hot water for 2 seconds to make removal easier. Place each on a plate and spoon the passionfruit pulp around the bases. Garnish and serve.

NUTRITION PER SERVE
Protein 8 g; Fat 2.5 g; Carbohydrate 10 g; Dietary Fibre 10 g; Cholesterol 3 mg; 455 kJ (110 cal)

Blend the strained passionfruit syrup, tofu, buttermilk, sugar and vanilla.

Sprinkle the gelatine over the surface of the water in the small bowl.

To remove, run a spatula around the edge and dip the base in hot water.

Strawberry and banana ice (top) and Passionfruit bavarois

CARROT CAKE WITH RICOTTA TOPPING

Fat per serve: 5 g
Preparation time: 20 minutes
Total cooking time: 1 hour 15 minutes
Makes 14 slices

2^1/2 cups (310 g/10 oz) self-
  raising flour
1 teaspoon bicarbonate of soda
2 teaspoons ground cinnamon
1 teaspoon mixed spice
^{1}/2 cup (95 g/3 oz) soft brown
  sugar
^{1}/2 cup (60 g/2 oz) sultanas
2 eggs, lightly beaten
2 tablespoons vegetable oil
^{1}/3 cup (80 ml/2^3/4 fl oz) low-fat
  milk
140 g (4^1/2 oz) apple purée
290 g (10 oz) carrot, coarsely
  grated

Ricotta topping
125 g (4 oz) ricotta
^{1}/4 cup (30 g/1 oz) icing sugar
^{1}/2 teaspoon grated lime rind

1 Preheat the oven to moderate 180°C (350°F/Gas 4). Lightly grease a 10 x 18 cm (4 x 7 inch) loaf tin and cover the base with baking paper. Sift the flour, soda and spices into a large bowl. Stir in the brown sugar and sultanas. Combine the eggs, oil, milk and apple purée in a large jug.
2 Stir the egg mixture into the dry ingredients, then stir in the carrot. Spread into the tin and bake for 1^1/4 hours, or until a skewer comes out clean when inserted in the centre of the cake and the cake comes away slightly from the sides of the tin. Leave in the tin for 5 minutes before turning out to cool on a wire rack.
3 To make the topping, beat the ingredients together until smooth. Spread over the cake.

NUTRITION PER SERVE
Protein 4.5 g; Fat 5 g; Carbohydrate 30 g; Dietary Fibre 2 g; Cholesterol 30 mg; 755 kJ (180 cal)

Stir the egg and apple mixture into the dry ingredients.

A skewer inserted into the centre of the cake should come out clean.

Beat the topping ingredients together until smooth.

BRAZIL NUT AND COFFEE BISCOTTI

Fat per serve: 1.5 g
Preparation time: 20 minutes
Total cooking time: 50 minutes
Makes 40

3 teaspoons instant coffee powder
1 tablespoon dark rum, warmed
2 eggs
1/2 cup (125 g/4 oz) caster sugar
1 1/4 cups (155 g/5 oz) plain flour
1/2 cup (60 g/2 oz) self-raising flour
1 teaspoon ground cinnamon
3/4 cup (105 g/3 1/2 oz) brazil nuts, roughly chopped
1 tablespoon caster sugar, extra

1 Preheat the oven to moderate 180°C (375°F/Gas 4). Dissolve the coffee in the rum. Beat the eggs and sugar until thick and creamy, then beat in the coffee mixture. Sift the flours and cinnamon into a bowl, then stir in the nuts. Mix in the egg mixture.

2 Divide the mixture into two rolls, each about 28 cm (11 inches) long. Line a baking tray with baking paper, put the rolls on it and press lightly to flatten them to about 6 cm (2 1/2 inches) across. Brush lightly with water and sprinkle with the extra sugar. Bake for 25 minutes, or until firm and light brown. Cool until warm on the tray. Reduce the oven temperature to warm 160°C (315°F/Gas 2–3).

3 Cut into 1 cm (1/2 inch) thick diagonal slices. Bake in a single layer on the lined tray for 20 minutes, or until dry, turning once. Cool on a rack. When cold, store in an airtight container for 2–3 weeks.

NUTRITION PER BISCOTTI
Protein 1 g; Fat 1.5 g; Carbohydrate 7.5 g; Dietary Fibre 0 g; Cholesterol 9 mg; 210 kJ (50 cal)

Beat the coffee and rum mixture into the beaten eggs and sugar.

Put the rolls of dough on the lined baking tray and press lightly into shape.

Cut the cooked rolls into diagonal slices and bake until dry.

Left to right: Oat and date;
Cornmeal and chilli;
Raisin, banana and apple;
Blueberry and almond;
Pumpkin and chive.

Muffins

In preparation for making any of these muffins, preheat the oven to moderately hot
200°C (400°F/Gas 6) and lightly spray a 12-hole muffin tin with cooking oil.
The holes should have a ¹/₂ cup (125 ml/4 fl oz) capacity.

OAT AND DATE

Sift 1 cup (125 g/4 oz) self-raising flour and 1 cup (125 g/4 oz) wholemeal self-raising flour with ¹/₂ teaspoon bicarbonate of soda into a large bowl. Return the husks to the bowl. Stir in 1 cup (100 g/3¹/₂ oz) quick rolled oats, ¹/₄ cup (55 g/2 oz) soft brown sugar and 1 cup (185 g/ 6 oz) chopped dates. Make a well in the centre. Beat together 1 egg, 2 tablespoons vegetable oil, ¹/₄ cup (90 g/3 oz) golden syrup and 1¹/₄ cups (310 ml/10 fl oz) skim milk in a jug. Pour into the dry ingredients and stir with a large metal spoon until just combined. The mixture will look lumpy. Do not overmix. Spoon into

the tin. Bake for 18 minutes, or until well risen and golden. Leave in the tin for 5 minutes before turning onto a wire rack to cool. Makes 12.

NUTRITION PER MUFFIN
Protein 5 g; Fat 5 g; Carbohydrate 15 g; Dietary Fibre 4 g; Cholesterol 15 mg; 910 kJ (220 cal)

CORNMEAL AND CHILLI

Combine 1 cup (150 g/5 oz) polenta and 1 tablespoon caster sugar in a large bowl. Sift together 1¹/₂ cups (185 g/6 oz) plain flour and 1 tablespoon baking powder and add to the bowl. Mix and make a well in the centre. Stir 2 tablespoons vegetable oil and 1 lightly beaten egg

with 1¹/₄ cups (315 ml/10 fl oz) skim milk in a jug, then pour onto the dry ingredients. Drain a 310 g (10 oz) can corn kernels and add to the mixture with 4 finely chopped spring onions and 1 finely chopped fresh small red chilli. Stir together with a large metal spoon until just combined. Do not overmix. Spoon into the tin. Sprinkle the tops with a little extra polenta. Bake for 20 minutes, or until well risen and golden brown. Leave the muffins in the tin for 5 minutes before turning onto a wire rack to cool. Makes 12.

NUTRITION PER MUFFIN
Protein 5 g; Fat 4 g; Carbohydrate 30 g; Dietary Fibre 2 g; Cholesterol 15 mg; 735 kJ (175 cal)

RAISIN, BANANA AND APPLE

Place 1 cup (200 g/6^{1}/2 oz) chopped raisins in a bowl, cover with boiling water, set aside for 30 minutes, then drain. Sift 1 cup (150 g/5 oz) wholemeal self-raising flour, 1 cup (125 g/4 oz) self-raising flour, 1 teaspoon ground cinnamon and ^{1}/2 cup (95 g/3 oz) soft brown sugar into a large bowl. Mix ^{1}/2 cup (135 g/4^{1}/2 oz) apple sauce, 1 egg and 1 cup (250 ml/8 fl oz) skim milk in a bowl. Stir in 2 tablespoons vegetable oil and a mashed banana. Stir the apple mixture and raisins into the flour with a large metal spoon until just combined. The mixture will look lumpy. Do not overmix. Spoon into the tin, sprinkle with 2 tablespoons rolled oats combined with 1 tablespoon soft brown sugar. Bake for 20 minutes, or until cooked through. Leave in the tin for 5 minutes before turning onto a wire rack to cool. Makes 12.

NUTRITION PER MUFFIN
Protein 4.5 g; Fat 4 g; Carbohydrate 40 g; Dietary Fibre 3 g; Cholesterol 15 mg; 880 kJ (210 cal)

BLUEBERRY AND ALMOND

Sift 2 cups (250 g/8 oz) self-raising flour into a large bowl. Stir in ^{1}/4 cup (60 g/2 oz) caster sugar and make a well in the centre. In a jug, combine 1 cup (250 ml/8 fl oz) skim milk, 1 lightly beaten egg, 1 teaspoon vanilla essence and 2 tablespoons melted polyunsaturated margarine. Pour into the dry ingredients and stir with a large metal spoon until just combined. The mixture will look lumpy. Do not overmix. Quickly stir through 200 g (6^{1}/2 oz) fresh blueberries. (Frozen blueberries can be used—add at the last minute while still frozen.) Spoon into the tin and sprinkle with 1 tablespoon demerara sugar combined with 30 g (1 oz) chopped almonds. Bake for 18 minutes, or until golden. Leave in the tin for 5 minutes before turning onto a wire rack to cool. Makes 12.

NUTRITION PER MUFFIN
Protein 3.5 g; Fat 3 g; Carbohydrate 25 g; Dietary Fibre 1 g; Cholesterol 15 mg; 595 kJ (145 cal)

PUMPKIN AND CHIVE

Combine 1 cup (250 g/8 oz) steamed and mashed pumpkin (375 g/12 oz uncooked, peeled), ^{3}/4 cup (185 ml/ 6 fl oz) skim milk, 2 tablespoons vegetable oil, 1 egg, 1 tablespoon soft brown sugar and ^{1}/4 teaspoon salt. Beat until smooth. Sift 1^{1}/4 cups (155 g/5 oz) self-raising flour and 1 cup (150 g/5 oz) wholemeal self-raising flour with ^{1}/2 teaspoon bicarbonate of soda into a large bowl. Return the husks to the bowl. Stir in 2 finely chopped spring onions, ^{1}/4 cup (15 g/^{1}/2 oz) chopped fresh chives and 2 tablespoons finely chopped fresh parsley. Make a well and pour in the liquid ingredients. Stir with a large metal spoon until just combined. The mixture will look lumpy. Do not overmix. Spoon into the tin. Sprinkle with fennel or dill seeds. Bake for 18 minutes, or until golden. Leave in the tin for 5 minutes before turning onto a wire rack to cool. Makes 12.

NUTRITION PER MUFFIN
Protein 4.5 g; Fat 4 g; Carbohydrate 20 g; Dietary Fibre 2 g; Cholesterol 15 mg; 550 kJ (130 cal)

TIRAMISU

Fat per serve: 5.5 g
Preparation time: 15 minutes
  + overnight refrigeration
Total cooking time: 5 minutes
Serves 6

3 tablespoons custard powder
1 cup (250 ml/8 fl oz) skim milk
2 tablespoons caster sugar
2 teaspoons vanilla essence
2 x 130 g (4$^{1}/_{2}$ oz) tubs light
    French Vanilla fruche or
    low-fat fromage frais
2 egg whites
1$^{2}/_{3}$ cups (410 ml/13 fl oz)
    prepared strong coffee, cooled
2 tablespoons amaretto
250 g (8 oz) Savoyardi
    (sponge finger) biscuits
2 tablespoons unsweetened dark
    cocoa powder

1 Stir the custard powder in a small pan with 2 tablespoons of the milk until dissolved. Add the remaining milk, sugar and vanilla and stir over medium heat until the mixture boils and thickens. Remove from the heat. This custard will be thicker than the usual custard. Transfer to a bowl, cover the surface with plastic wrap and cool at room temperature.

2 Using electric beaters, mix the custard and the fruche in a bowl. Beat for 2 minutes. In a small bowl, whip the egg whites until soft peaks form, then fold into the custard mixture.

3 Pour the coffee into a dish and add the amaretto. Quickly dip the biscuits, one at a time, in the coffee mixture, just enough to cover (don't leave them in the liquid or they will go soggy) and arrange in a single layer over the base of a 2.75 litre capacity serving dish.

4 Using half the cream mixture, smooth it evenly over the biscuits. Dust half the dark cocoa over the cream and then repeat the layers with the remaining biscuits and cream. Cover with plastic wrap. Refrigerate overnight, or for at least 6 hours. Dust with dark cocoa powder to serve.

NUTRITION PER SERVE
Protein 5 g; Fat 5.5 g; Carbohydrate 26 g;
Dietary Fibre 1 g; Cholesterol 7.5 mg;
754 kJ (180 cal)

Stir the custard powder in a small amount of milk until dissolved.

Fold the whipped egg whites into the custard mixture.

Dip the biscuits quickly into the coffee mixture to cover evenly.

Use a strainer to dust half the cocoa over the cream.

CREAMY RICE POTS

Fat per serve: 3.5 g
Preparation time: 15 minutes
Total cooking time: 1 hour
Serves 4

1/2 cup (110 g/3 1/2 oz) short-
  grain rice
1 litre skim milk
1/4 cup (60 g/2 oz) caster sugar
1 teaspoon grated orange rind
1 teaspoon grated lemon rind
1 teaspoon vanilla essence
20 g (3/4 oz) hazelnuts
1 tablespoon soft brown sugar

1 Wash the short-grain rice in a sieve under running water for a few seconds, then drain thoroughly. Combine the skim milk and caster sugar in a non-stick pan and stir over low heat until the sugar has completely dissolved. Add the rice and rind and stir briefly to distribute. Bring to the boil and reduce the heat to as low as possible. Cook for 1 hour, stirring occasionally, until the rice is tender and the mixture is thick and creamy. Stir in the vanilla essence.

2 While the rice is cooking, spread the hazelnuts on a baking tray and toast in a moderate 180°C (350°F/ Gas 4) oven for about 5 minutes. Rub the hot nuts in a tea towel to remove as much of the skin as possible. Cool and then grind in a food processor to a coarse texture, not too fine. Preheat a grill to very hot.

3 Spoon the rice into 4 heatproof 3/4 cup (185 ml/6 fl oz) capacity ramekins. Combine the brown sugar and ground hazelnuts and sprinkle over the surface of the rice. Cook briefly under the grill until the sugar melts and the nuts are lightly browned. Serve immediately.

NUTRITION PER SERVE
Protein 12 g; Fat 3.5 g; Carbohydrate 55 g; Dietary Fibre 1 g; Cholesterol 7 mg; 1235 kJ (295 cal)

Cook the rice mixture over very low heat until thick and creamy.

Transfer the hot nuts to a tea towel and rub to remove as much skin as possible.

Sprinkle the combined sugar and ground hazelnuts over the top of the rice.

PASSIONFRUIT TART

Fat per serve: 6.5 g
Preparation time: 25 minutes
 + 30 minutes refrigeration
Total cooking time: 1 hour
Serves 8

³/4 cup (90 g/3 oz) plain flour
2 tablespoons icing sugar
2 tablespoons custard powder
30 g (1 oz) butter
3 tablespoons light evaporated
 milk

Filling
¹/2 cup (125 g/4 oz) ricotta
1 teaspoon vanilla essence
¹/4 cup (30 g/1 oz) icing sugar
2 eggs, lightly beaten
4 tablespoons passionfruit pulp
 (about 8 passionfruit)
³/4 cup (185 ml/6 fl oz) light
 evaporated milk

1 Preheat the oven to moderately hot 200°C (400°F/Gas 6). Lightly spray a 22 cm (9 inch) loose-based flan tin with oil spray. Sift the flour, icing sugar and custard powder into a bowl and rub in the butter until the mixture resembles fine breadcrumbs. Add enough evaporated milk to form a soft dough. Bring together on a lightly floured surface until just smooth. Gather into a ball, wrap in plastic and refrigerate for 15 minutes.
2 Roll the pastry out on a floured surface, to fit the tin, then refrigerate for 15 minutes. Cover with baking paper and fill with uncooked rice or beans. Bake for 10 minutes, remove the rice or beans and paper and bake for another 5–8 minutes, or until golden. Allow to cool. Reduce the

oven to warm 160°C (315°F/Gas 2–3).
3 Beat the ricotta with the vanilla essence and icing sugar until smooth. Add the eggs, passionfruit pulp and milk, then beat well. Put the tin with the pastry case on a baking tray and gently pour in the mixture. Bake for

40 minutes, or until set. Allow to cool in the tin. Dust lightly with icing sugar just before serving.

NUTRITION PER SERVE
Protein 8 g; Fat 6.5 g; Carbohydrate 25 g; Dietary Fibre 3 g; Cholesterol 65 mg; 750 kJ (180 cal)

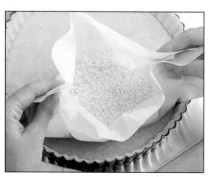

Remove the baking paper and uncooked rice or beans.

When the ricotta mixture is smooth, add the eggs, passionfruit pulp and milk.

Put the tin on a baking tray and gently pour in the filling.

FIGS WITH ORANGE CREAM AND RAISINS

Fat per serve: 3.5 g
Preparation time: 20 minutes
  + 1 hour soaking
Total cooking time: 12 minutes
Serves 4

1 cup (125 g/4 oz) raisins
75 ml (2¹/2 fl oz) tawny port
1 tablespoon custard powder
1 cup (250 ml/8 fl oz) skim milk
1 tablespoon sugar
100 g (3¹/2 oz) ricotta
200 g (6¹/2 oz) light French
  Vanilla Fruche or low-fat
  fromage frais

rind strips and juice of 1 orange
1 teaspoon ground cinnamon
8 fresh figs

1 Soak the raisins in the tawny port for 1 hour, or until plumped up.
2 In a small saucepan, blend the custard powder with the skim milk, add the sugar and stir over low heat until the sugar has dissolved. Increase the heat to medium and stir continuously until the custard boils and thickens. Remove from the heat immediately, pour into a small bowl and cover with plastic wrap. Cool completely. When cooled, transfer to the small bowl of an electric mixer, add the ricotta and fruche and beat until smooth.

3 Just before serving, warm the raisin mixture with the orange rind, juice and cinnamon in a small pan, over low heat, for 2–3 minutes. Cover and keep warm.
4 Starting from the top, cut the figs into quarters, slicing only two-thirds of the way down so the figs hold together. Transfer the figs to ramekins or a serving dish or platter. Place 2 heaped tablespoons of the custard cream mixture into the centre of each fig, top with a spoonful of the warm raisin and orange mixture and serve at once.

NUTRITION PER SERVE
Protein 7 g; Fat 3.5 g; Carbohydrate 45 g; Dietary Fibre 4.5 g; Cholesterol 15 mg; 1510 kJ (360 cal)

Stir the custard continuously until it boils and thickens.

When the custard has cooled, combine it with the ricotta and fruche in a bowl.

Cut the figs into quarters, slicing only two-thirds of the way down.

ALMOND AND PEAR POUCHES

Fat per serve: 7 g
Preparation time: 45 minutes
  + 10 minutes standing
Total cooking time: 40 minutes
Makes 4

4 beurre bosc (or any firm) pears
$^1/_4$ cup (60 ml/2 fl oz) white wine
$^1/_4$ cup (60 g/2 oz) caster sugar
1 cinnamon stick
2 cloves
1 vanilla bean
4 dates, roughly chopped
2 tablespoons sultanas
$^2/_3$ cup (85 g/3 oz) plain flour
1 egg, lightly beaten
1 cup (250 ml/8 fl oz) skim milk
2 tablespoons ground almonds
1 tablespoon soft brown sugar
$^1/_2$ teaspoon ground cinnamon
2 teaspoons flaked almonds
icing sugar, for dusting

Strawberry sauce
125 g (4 oz) strawberries,
  chopped
1 teaspoon caster sugar
2 tablespoons orange juice

1 Remove the cores of the pears through the base using a melon baller, then peel. Combine 2 cups (500 ml/ 16 fl oz) water with the wine, sugar, cinnamon stick and cloves in a pan that is just large enough to fit the pears. Split the vanilla bean in half lengthways and scrape the seeds out. Add to the pan with the vanilla pod and stir over medium heat until the sugar has dissolved.
2 Add the pears to the pan and simmer, covered, for 20 minutes, or until just soft when tested with a skewer. Remove from the heat and allow to cool in the syrup. Drain and stand the pears on paper towels. Fill the base of each with the combined dates and sultanas.
3 To make the crepes, sift the flour into a bowl, gradually beat in the combined egg and milk, beating until smooth. Strain into a jug and set aside for 10 minutes.
4 Preheat the oven to moderately hot 200°C (400°F/Gas 6). Lightly oil a 24 cm (9$^1/_2$ inch) non-stick pan with oil spray, heat the pan and pour in a quarter of the batter, swirling to cover the base of the pan. Cook until lightly browned, turn and brown the other side. Remove and repeat with the remaining mixture.
5 Place the crepes on a work bench, place a quarter of the combined ground almonds, brown sugar and cinnamon in the centre of each and top with a pear. Gather the crepes around the pears and tie with string. Sprinkle with the flaked almonds. Bake on a lightly oiled baking tray for 5 minutes, or until the almonds and the edges of the crepes are golden and the pears just warm. Discard the string. To make the strawberry sauce, blend the strawberries, sugar and orange juice in a blender until smooth, then strain.
6 Dust the pear pouches with a little icing sugar and serve with strawberry sauce. For a special effect, you can tie a piece of raffia or ribbon around each pouch before serving.

NUTRITION PER SERVE
Protein 9.5 g; Fat 7 g; Carbohydrate 80 g; Dietary Fibre 7 g; Cholesterol 45 mg; 1740 kJ (415 cal)

Use a melon baller to remove the cores from the pears through the bases.

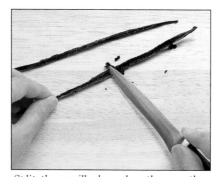

Split the vanilla bean lengthways, then scrape the seeds out with a knife.

Combine the dates and sultanas and fill the base of each pear.

Heat the pan and pour in a quarter of the batter, swirling to cover the base.

Put the ground almonds, sugar and cinnamon mix on the pancakes.

Gather the crepes around the pears and tie with string.

BANANA PANCAKES

Fat per serve: 0.5 g
Preparation time: 20 minutes + standing
Total cooking time: 25 minutes
Makes 10

2 very ripe bananas, mashed
1 cup (150 g/5 oz) wholemeal
 flour
2 teaspoons baking powder
1/2 teaspoon ground cinnamon
pinch of ground nutmeg
1 cup (250 ml/8 fl oz) skim milk
1 tablespoon maple syrup

maple syrup and slices of
 banana, for serving

1 Put the mashed banana in a large bowl. Sift the flour, baking powder, cinnamon and nutmeg onto the banana and return the husks to the bowl. Stir until the flour is moistened but not totally combined with the banana.
2 Make a well in the centre, add the milk and syrup and stir constantly until smooth. Set aside for 1 hour.
3 Heat a large non-stick pan over medium heat and coat with cooking oil spray. Cook the pancakes in batches, using 1/4 cup (60 ml/2 fl oz) of

batter for each pancake. Cook for 3–4 minutes, or until small bubbles appear on the surface. Using a spatula, gently turn the pancakes over, loosening the edges first so they don't stick to the pan. Cook for another 3 minutes. Remove from the pan and keep warm. Spray the pan with a little oil after each batch and continue with the remaining mixture. Serve drizzled with maple syrup and a few slices of banana.

NUTRITION PER PANCAKE
Protein 3 g; Fat 0.5 g; Carbohydrate 17 g;
Dietary Fibre 2 g; Cholesterol 1 mg;
350 kJ (85 cal)

When the flour is sifted, return the husks to the bowl.

Stir the pancake mixture until smooth, then set aside for 1 hour.

Cook the pancakes over medium heat until small bubbles appear on the surface.

Beat the sugar and eggs together until light and fluffy.

Slowly fold the flour, in small batches, into the mixture.

Once the cakes are completely cooled, slice in half horizontally.

When the cakes are joined with the chestnut mixture, cut out heart shapes.

CHESTNUT HEARTS

Fat per serve: 1 g
Preparation time: 40 minutes
Total cooking time: 40 minutes
Makes 30

2/3 cup (160 g/5 1/2 oz) caster
  sugar
2 eggs
2 1/2 teaspoons coconut essence
6 egg whites
1 teaspoon cream of tartar
1 1/4 cups (155 g/5 oz) self-
  raising flour, sifted
1 cup (250 g/8 oz) canned
  sweetened chestnut purée
1/3 cup (90 g/3 oz) ricotta
2 teaspoons cocoa powder
icing sugar, to dust

1 Preheat the oven to moderate 180°C (350°F/Gas 4). Lightly spray two 20 x 30 cm (8 x 12 inch) shallow baking tins with oil spray and line the base and sides with baking paper.
2 To make the sponge, beat the sugar and eggs in a bowl with electric beaters for 3–4 minutes, until light and fluffy. Transfer to a large bowl. Add the coconut essence and transfer to a larger bowl.
3 Beat the egg whites until foamy. Add the cream of tartar and beat until firm peaks form. Stir a third of the egg white into the creamed mixture. Slowly fold in the flour in small batches, alternating with small amounts of egg white. Fold in both until just combined. Divide the mixture between the trays. Bake for 20–25 minutes, until golden. Test with a skewer. Turn out onto cooling racks lined with greaseproof paper. Cool thoroughly. If possible, bake ahead and store in an airtight container.
4 In a blender, mix the chestnut purée with the ricotta and cocoa until very smooth. Slice the cakes in half horizontally and join with the chestnut mixture. Cut out heart shapes using a heart-shaped cookie cutter, about 5.5 cm (2 1/4 inches) across and 4.5 cm (1 3/4 inches) long. Clean the cutter between cuts or dust it in icing sugar if the cake sticks. Dust with icing sugar before serving.

NUTRITION PER SERVE
Protein 1 g; Fat 1 g; Carbohydrate 8 g; Dietary Fibre 0.5 g; Cholesterol 8.5 mg; 175 kJ (40 cal)

MANGO PASSIONFRUIT SORBET

Fat per serve: Nil
Preparation time: 20 minutes
  + 8 hours freezing
Total cooking time: 5 minutes
Serves 6

1 cup (250 g/8 oz) caster sugar
1/3 cup (90 g/3 oz) passionfruit
  pulp
1/2 large mango (200 g/6 1/2 oz),
  chopped
1 large (250 g/8 oz) peach,
  chopped
2 tablespoons lemon juice
1 egg white

1 Stir the sugar in a pan with 1 cup (250 ml/8 fl oz) water over low heat until dissolved. Increase the heat, bring to the boil and boil for 1 minute. Transfer to a glass bowl, cool, then refrigerate. Strain the passionfruit pulp, reserving 1 tablespoon of the seeds.
2 Blend the fruit, passionfruit juice and lemon juice in a blender until smooth. With the motor running, add the cold sugar syrup and 150 ml (5 fl oz) water. Stir in the passionfruit seeds. Freeze in a shallow container, stirring occasionally, for about 5 hours, or until almost set.
3 Break up the icy mixture roughly with a fork or spoon, transfer to a bowl and beat with electric beaters until smooth and fluffy. Beat the egg white in a small bowl until firm peaks form, then fold into the mixture until just combined. Spread into a loaf tin and return to the freezer until firm. Transfer to the refrigerator, to soften, 15 minutes before serving.

NUTRITION PER SERVE
Protein 2 g; Fat 0 g; Carbohydrate 50 g; Dietary Fibre 3 g; Cholesterol 0 mg; 850 kJ (200 cal)

COOK'S FILE

Hint: You will need about 1 large mango, 6 passionfruit and 3 or 4 peaches for this recipe.
Variation: To make a berry sorbet, use 200 g (6 1/2 oz) blackberries or blueberries, 200 g (6 1/2 oz) hulled strawberries and 50 g (1 3/4 oz) peach flesh. Prepare as above.

Leave the motor running and pour in the cold sugar syrup and water.

Gently fold the egg white into the smooth fruit purée.

BANANA AND BLUEBERRY TART

Fat per serve: 6 g
Preparation time: 30 minutes
Total cooking time: 25 minutes
Serves 6

cooking oil spray
1 cup (125 g/4 oz) plain flour
1/2 cup (60 g/2 oz) self-raising flour
1 teaspoon cinnamon
1 teaspoon ground ginger
40 g (1 1/4 oz) butter, chopped

1/2 cup (95 g/3 oz) soft brown sugar
1/2 cup (125 ml/4 oz) buttermilk
200 g (6 1/2 oz) blueberries
2 bananas
2 teaspoons lemon juice
1 tablespoon demerara sugar

1 Preheat the oven to moderately hot 200°C (400°F/Gas 6). Spray a baking tray or pizza tray lightly with oil. Sift the flours and spices into a bowl. Add the butter and sugar and rub in until the mixture resembles breadcrumbs. Make a well and then add enough buttermilk to mix to a soft dough.

2 Roll the dough out on a lightly floured surface to a 23 cm (9 inch) diameter round. Place on the tray and roll the edge to form a lip to hold the fruit in.

3 Spread the blueberries over the dough, keeping within the lip. Slice the bananas, toss them in the lemon juice, then arrange over the top. Sprinkle with the sugar, and bake for 25 minutes, until the base is browned. Serve immediately.

NUTRITION PER SERVE
Protein 5 g; Fat 6 g; Carbohydrate 55 g; Dietary Fibre 3 g; Cholesterol 20 mg; 1215 kJ (290 cal)

Rub the butter into the flour mix using your fingertips.

Pour in the buttermilk, using enough to form a soft dough.

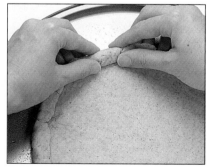

Put the circle of dough on the tray and roll the edge to form a lip.

FRUIT JELLIES

Fat per serve: Nil
Preparation time: 20 minutes
  + refrigeration
Total cooking time: Nil
Serves 4

4 teaspoons gelatine
2 cups (500 ml/16 fl oz)
  cranberry and raspberry juice
330 g (11 oz) mixed berries,
  fresh or frozen

1 Sprinkle the gelatine in an even layer onto 3 tablespoons of the juice, in a small bowl, and leave to go spongy. Bring a small pan of water to the boil, remove from the heat and place the bowl in the pan. The water should come halfway up the side of the bowl. Stir the gelatine until clear and dissolved. Cool slightly and mix with the rest of the juice.

2 Rinse four ³/4 cup (185 ml/6 fl oz) moulds with water (wet moulds make it easier when unmoulding) and pour 2 cm (³/4 inch) of the juice into each. Refrigerate until set. Meanwhile, if the fruit is frozen, defrost it and add any liquid to the remaining juice. When the bottom layer of jelly has set, divide the fruit among the moulds (reserving a few berries to garnish) and divide the rest of the juice among the moulds, pouring it over the fruit. Refrigerate until set.

3 To turn out the jellies, hold each mould in a hot, damp tea towel and turn out onto a plate. Ease away the edge of the jelly with your finger to break the seal. (If you turn the jellies onto a damp plate you will be able to move them around, otherwise they will stick.) Garnish with the reserved berries.

NUTRITION PER SERVE
Protein 3 g; Fat 0 g; Carbohydrate 25 g; Dietary Fibre 1.5 g; Cholesterol 0 mg; 420 kJ (100 cal)

Lower the gelatine bowl into the water and stir the gelatine until dissolved.

Divide the fruit among the moulds and pour in the rest of the juice.

Use your finger to ease away the edge of the jelly to break the seal.

INDEX

INTERNATIONAL GLOSSARY OF INGREDIENTS

baby squash	pattypan squash	coriander	cilantro	self-raising flour	self-rising flour
bicarbonate of soda	baking soda	cornflour	cornstarch	semi-dried	sun-blushed
bok choy	pak choi, pak choy	eggplant	aubergine	silverbeet	Swiss chard
		flat-leaf parsley	Italian parsley	snow pea	mangetout
broad beans	fava beans	icing sugar	confectioners' sugar	soft brown sugar	light brown sugar
butternut pumpkin	squash	mince	ground meat	spring onion	scallion
		plain flour	all-purpose flour	tomato paste (Aus./US)	tomato purée/double concentrate (UK)
capsicum	pepper	polenta	cornmeal	tomato purée (Aus.)	passata/sieved
caster sugar	superfine sugar	prawn, raw	shrimp, green		crushed tomatoes (UK)
chickpeas	garbanzo beans	rocket	arugula		
chilli	chile, chili pepper	Roma tomato	plum tomato	zucchini	courgette

This edition published in 2008 by Bay Books, an imprint of Murdoch Books Pty Limited.
Pier 8/9, 23 Hickson Road, Millers Point, NSW 2000, Australia.

Managing Editor: Rachel Carter **Editor:** Wendy Stephen **Designer:** Norman Baptista **Editorial Assistant:** Stephanie Kistner **Food Director:** Jody Vassallo **Food Editor:** Kathy Knudsen **Recipe Development:** Anna Beaumont, Alex Diblasi, Michelle Earl, Lulu Grimes, Kathy Knudsen, Michelle Lawton, Beth Mitchell, Justine Poole, Kerrie Ray **Nutritionist:** Thérèse Abbey **Photographers:** Andre Martin, Reg Morrison (steps) **Food Stylist:** Marie Hélène Clauzon **Food Preparation:** Kerrie Mullins **Chief Executive:** Juliet Rogers **Publisher:** Kay Scarlett

The nutritional information provided for each recipe does not include garnishes or accompaniments, such as rice, unless they are included in specific quantities in the ingredients. The values are approximations and can be affected by biological and seasonal variations in food, the unknown composition of some manufactured foods and uncertainty in the dietary database. Nutrient data given are derived primarily from the NUTTAB95 database produced by the Australian New Zealand Food Authority.

ISBN: 978 0 681 24488 7
Printed by Sing Cheong Printing Co. Ltd. PRINTED IN CHINA.